AI and OSINT: The Future of Cyber Investigation

Matteo Schubert

About the Author

Matteo Schubert is a seasoned cybersecurity expert and a leading authority in the field of Open Source Intelligence (OSINT). With over a decade of experience in cyber investigations, Matteo has earned a reputation for his deep understanding of the intersection between technology and intelligence. His work has spanned across multiple domains, including corporate security, law enforcement, and national defense, where he has applied cutting-edge techniques to unravel complex cyber threats.

Matteo holds a degree in Computer Science and advanced certifications in cybersecurity, which have equipped him with the technical expertise to navigate the rapidly evolving landscape of digital security. His passion for innovation has driven him to explore the potential of Artificial Intelligence (AI) in enhancing OSINT practices, leading to groundbreaking advancements in automated threat detection and analysis.

As a prolific author and speaker, Matteo has contributed extensively to the cybersecurity community, sharing his insights through numerous publications, workshops, and conferences. His commitment to education and mentorship has inspired countless professionals to pursue excellence in cyber investigations and intelligence gathering.

In "AI and OSINT: The Future of Cyber Investigation," Matteo brings together his vast knowledge and practical experience to offer a comprehensive guide on the transformative power of AI in the world of OSINT. This book is a culmination of his years of research and hands-on work, providing readers with valuable tools and strategies to stay ahead in the ever-changing realm of cybersecurity.

When he's not delving into the latest cyber trends, Matteo enjoys exploring the outdoors, practicing martial arts, and spending time with his family. He continues to push the boundaries of what's possible in cybersecurity, always looking for the next innovation that will shape the future of digital intelligence.

In an era where digital information proliferates at an unprecedented rate, the need for advanced cyber investigation techniques has never been more critical. Open Source Intelligence (OSINT) has long been a cornerstone of cyber investigations, providing valuable insights by collecting and analyzing publicly available data. However, as the volume and complexity of data have grown, so too has the demand for more sophisticated tools to harness this information effectively.

This is where Artificial Intelligence (AI) comes into play. By automating and enhancing OSINT processes, AI has the potential to revolutionize how we approach cyber investigations. From real-time threat detection to predictive analytics, AI-driven OSINT offers unparalleled opportunities to stay ahead of cybercriminals and protect critical assets.

"**AI and OSINT: The Future of Cyber Investigation**" is a comprehensive guide that explores the transformative power of AI in the realm of OSINT. Whether you are a cybersecurity professional, a law enforcement officer, or simply someone interested in the future of digital intelligence, this book provides you with the knowledge and tools needed to navigate this rapidly evolving field.

Chapter Summary

Chapter 1: Introduction to AI and OSINT

The opening chapter provides an overview of AI and OSINT, setting the stage for the discussions that follow. It explores the synergy between these two fields and explains why their integration is crucial for modern cyber investigations.

Chapter 2: The Evolution of OSINT in Cybersecurity

This chapter traces the history of OSINT, highlighting its role in early cybersecurity efforts. It examines traditional OSINT techniques, their limitations, and the pressing need for AI to overcome these challenges.

Chapter 3: AI Techniques for Enhancing OSINT

Dive into the specific AI techniques that are enhancing OSINT practices. From machine learning and natural language processing to image recognition and anomaly detection, this chapter explores how AI is being applied to extract actionable intelligence from vast data sources.

Chapter 4: OSINT Tools Powered by AI

This chapter provides a detailed look at the AI-driven tools currently shaping the OSINT landscape. It includes a comparative analysis of popular tools, their key features, and case studies demonstrating their effectiveness in real-world investigations.

Chapter 5: Real-Time Threat Intelligence

Explore the role of AI in real-time threat intelligence, focusing on its applications in monitoring social media, analyzing dark web activities, and detecting emerging cyber threats. This chapter underscores the importance of staying ahead in a constantly evolving threat landscape.

Chapter 6: AI-Driven Automation in Cyber Investigations

Learn how AI is automating key aspects of cyber investigations, from data collection to analysis. This chapter discusses the benefits and challenges of AI-driven automation and how to strike a balance between human expertise and machine efficiency.

Chapter 7: Ethical Considerations in AI and OSINT

As AI becomes more integrated into OSINT, ethical considerations become increasingly important. This chapter addresses privacy concerns, algorithmic bias, and the need for transparency and accountability in AI applications.

Chapter 8: Legal and Regulatory Frameworks

Understanding the legal implications of AI in OSINT is crucial for compliance and ethical practice. This chapter covers global regulations, data protection laws, and best practices for navigating the complex legal landscape of AI-driven investigations.

Chapter 9: Case Studies: AI in Action

Real-world case studies bring the concepts discussed in previous chapters to life. This chapter presents successful and failed AI-OSINT integrations, offering lessons learned and insights into future applications.

Chapter 10: The Future of AI and OSINT

Looking ahead, this chapter explores emerging technologies and trends that will shape the future of AI and OSINT. It discusses how these advancements will impact cyber investigations and what professionals can do to prepare for the next wave of innovations.

Chapter 11: Practical Implementation and Challenges

For those looking to integrate AI into their OSINT workflows, this chapter provides a practical guide. It covers the steps for implementation, common challenges, and strategies for building a successful AI-OSINT strategy within an organization.

Chapter 1: Introduction to AI and OSINT

Chapter 1, "Introduction to AI and OSINT," sets the stage by exploring the foundational concepts of Artificial Intelligence (AI) and Open Source Intelligence (OSINT), two pivotal forces in modern cyber investigations. This chapter introduces the symbiotic relationship between AI and OSINT, illustrating how their convergence is transforming the way we gather and analyze information in the digital age. As cyber threats become more sophisticated, understanding the basics of AI and OSINT is essential for leveraging these technologies to uncover, prevent, and respond to malicious activities.

1.1. Defining Artificial Intelligence (AI)

Artificial Intelligence (AI) is a multidisciplinary field of computer science dedicated to creating systems capable of performing tasks that typically require human intelligence. These tasks include learning from experience, understanding natural language, recognizing patterns, solving complex problems, and making decisions. AI's aim is to develop machines that can mimic human cognitive functions and improve their performance over time through learning and adaptation.

The Concept of AI

At its core, AI is about developing algorithms and models that enable machines to perform tasks that usually necessitate human intelligence. This can involve a variety of cognitive functions, such as reasoning, perception, and problem-solving. The field of AI can be broadly divided into two categories: narrow AI and general AI.

Narrow AI, also known as weak AI, is designed to perform specific tasks or solve particular problems. Most AI applications in use today fall under this category. Examples include virtual assistants like Siri and Alexa, recommendation systems on platforms like Netflix and Amazon, and image recognition systems used in social media. These systems are highly specialized and optimized for their designated functions but lack the ability to generalize their knowledge or perform tasks beyond their specific design.

General AI, also referred to as strong AI or AGI (Artificial General Intelligence), aims to create systems with generalized human cognitive abilities. This type of AI would possess the capacity to understand, learn, and apply knowledge across a broad range of tasks in a manner comparable to human intelligence. AGI remains a theoretical concept and is a subject of ongoing research and debate within the AI community.

Core Components of AI

To understand AI fully, it's important to examine its core components:

Machine Learning (ML): ML is a subset of AI focused on developing algorithms that allow machines to learn from and make predictions or decisions based on data. Unlike traditional programming, where explicit instructions are given, ML systems improve their performance by identifying patterns and making data-driven predictions. ML encompasses various approaches, including supervised learning, unsupervised learning, and reinforcement learning.

Supervised Learning involves training a model on labeled data, where the desired outputs are known. The model learns to map inputs to the correct outputs by finding patterns in the training data.

Unsupervised Learning deals with unlabeled data, where the system tries to identify hidden patterns or structures within the data. Techniques such as clustering and dimensionality reduction are commonly used in this approach.

Reinforcement Learning is based on the concept of learning through interaction with an environment. An agent learns to make decisions by receiving rewards or penalties based on its actions, thereby improving its strategy over time.

Natural Language Processing (NLP): NLP enables machines to understand, interpret, and generate human language. It involves various tasks, such as speech recognition, language translation, sentiment analysis, and text summarization. NLP combines computational linguistics, statistical modeling, and machine learning to process and analyze large volumes of text data.

Computer Vision: Computer vision focuses on enabling machines to interpret and understand visual information from the world. It involves tasks such as image recognition, object detection, and image segmentation. Computer vision algorithms analyze and extract features from images or videos to make sense of visual data.

Robotics: Robotics involves the design and development of robots that can perform physical tasks. AI plays a crucial role in enabling robots to perceive their environment, make decisions, and act autonomously. Robotics applications range from industrial automation to autonomous vehicles.

Expert Systems: Expert systems are AI applications designed to emulate the decision-making ability of human experts in specific domains. They use a knowledge base of domain-specific information and inference rules to provide solutions or recommendations.

Historical Evolution of AI

AI as a field has evolved significantly since its inception. The concept of AI dates back to ancient times, with early philosophical inquiries into the nature of intelligence and reasoning. However, modern AI research began in the mid-20th century with the advent of digital computers and the development of formal logic.

1950s: Alan Turing proposed the concept of a machine that could simulate any human intelligence and introduced the Turing Test as a measure of a machine's ability to exhibit intelligent behavior. The Dartmouth Conference in 1956, organized by John McCarthy, is often considered the birth of AI as a formal field of study.

1960s-1970s: Early AI research focused on symbolic reasoning and problem-solving. Early successes included solving mathematical problems and playing games like chess. However, limitations in computational power and the complexity of real-world tasks led to a period of reduced funding and interest, known as the "AI winter."

1980s-1990s: The development of expert systems and improved algorithms reignited interest in AI. Expert systems like MYCIN demonstrated the potential of AI in specific domains, such as medical diagnosis. The emergence of machine learning techniques and increased computational power further advanced the field.

2000s-Present: The advent of big data and advanced machine learning techniques, such as deep learning, has led to significant breakthroughs in AI. The success of AI systems in areas like image recognition, natural language processing, and game playing has brought AI into mainstream applications, including virtual assistants, autonomous vehicles, and personalized recommendations.

AI's Impact and Future

AI's impact on society and various industries is profound and far-reaching. It has the potential to transform how we work, live, and interact with technology. AI applications are being used to enhance healthcare, improve transportation, optimize business processes, and address complex scientific problems.

However, the rise of AI also raises important ethical and societal considerations. Issues such as privacy, security, bias, and the future of work are critical topics that require careful consideration as AI technologies continue to evolve.

The future of AI holds exciting possibilities, including advances in AGI, improvements in human-AI collaboration, and innovations that address global challenges. As AI continues to advance, it will be essential to balance technological progress with ethical and societal considerations to ensure that AI benefits all of humanity.

In summary, Artificial Intelligence is a dynamic and rapidly evolving field that aims to create systems capable of performing tasks that require human-like intelligence. From its early conceptualizations to its current applications and future prospects, AI represents a transformative technology with the potential to shape the future of many aspects of our lives.

1.2. Understanding Open Source Intelligence (OSINT)

Open Source Intelligence (OSINT) is a crucial aspect of modern intelligence and investigative work that involves collecting, analyzing, and utilizing information obtained from publicly available sources. Unlike classified or proprietary intelligence, OSINT relies on data that is freely accessible and legally obtainable by anyone. This chapter explores the nature of OSINT, its methodologies, applications, and the role it plays in various fields such as cybersecurity, law enforcement, and competitive analysis.

Defining OSINT

OSINT refers to the process of gathering and analyzing information from openly available sources to support decision-making and provide actionable insights. These sources can include, but are not limited to:

- **Publicly Accessible Internet Resources**: Websites, blogs, forums, social media platforms, and online databases.
- **Traditional Media**: Newspapers, magazines, radio, and television broadcasts.
- **Government Publications**: Official reports, press releases, and statistical data.
- **Academic Publications**: Research papers, journals, and conference proceedings.
- **Commercial Data**: Market research reports, industry analyses, and business directories.

The primary goal of OSINT is to gather information that is relevant, accurate, and useful for achieving specific objectives, whether for security, investigative, or business purposes.

The OSINT Process

The OSINT process typically involves several key steps:

Planning and Preparation: Define the objectives of the intelligence gathering effort and determine the types of information needed. This step includes identifying the sources to be monitored and setting up a strategy for data collection and analysis.

Data Collection: Gather information from selected sources. This can involve web scraping, manual searches, social media monitoring, and accessing public records. The aim is to collect as much relevant data as possible while ensuring its authenticity and credibility.

Data Analysis: Analyze the collected data to extract meaningful insights. This may involve organizing, correlating, and interpreting the information to identify patterns, trends, and potential threats. Analytical techniques can include statistical analysis, content analysis, and geospatial analysis.

Reporting and Dissemination: Prepare and present the findings in a clear and actionable format. This can include written reports, presentations, or visualizations that highlight key insights and recommendations. The final output should be tailored to the needs of the intended audience.

Evaluation and Feedback: Assess the effectiveness of the OSINT effort and gather feedback to refine future intelligence-gathering activities. This step involves reviewing the accuracy and relevance of the information obtained and making adjustments to the process as needed.

Key Characteristics of OSINT

Legality: OSINT relies on information that is legally accessible to the public. Unlike other forms of intelligence, it does not involve covert or classified sources. This makes OSINT a transparent and ethical approach to information gathering.

Accessibility: The information used in OSINT is readily available through various channels. With the proliferation of digital platforms and online resources, accessing and retrieving open-source data has become increasingly straightforward.

Variety: OSINT encompasses a wide range of sources and types of information. This diversity allows for a comprehensive understanding of the subject matter and can provide a well-rounded perspective on the intelligence being gathered.

Timeliness: OSINT can provide real-time or near-real-time insights, especially when monitoring dynamic sources such as social media. This timeliness is valuable for addressing immediate issues or emerging threats.

Applications of OSINT

OSINT is employed across various domains, each leveraging its capabilities for specific purposes:

Cybersecurity: In cybersecurity, OSINT is used to identify potential threats, monitor cyber activities, and analyze vulnerabilities. By examining publicly available data such as hacker forums, threat reports, and social media, cybersecurity professionals can gain insights into emerging threats and vulnerabilities.

Law Enforcement: Law enforcement agencies use OSINT to support criminal investigations, track suspects, and gather evidence. Social media and public records are often used to gather information about criminal activities, connections, and locations.

Competitive Intelligence: Businesses use OSINT to gain insights into market trends, competitor activities, and industry developments. This information helps organizations make informed decisions about strategic planning, market positioning, and risk management.

National Security: OSINT plays a role in national security by providing intelligence on geopolitical events, terrorist activities, and other global issues. Governments and intelligence agencies use OSINT to monitor open sources for information relevant to national security interests.

Academic and Research: Researchers and academics use OSINT to gather data for studies, literature reviews, and public opinion analysis. Open access to academic publications, government reports, and industry data supports a wide range of research activities.

Challenges and Considerations

While OSINT offers numerous benefits, it also comes with its own set of challenges:

Data Overload: The sheer volume of available information can be overwhelming. Effective OSINT requires filtering and prioritizing relevant data to avoid information overload.

Data Quality and Accuracy: Not all publicly available information is accurate or reliable. Verifying the credibility and authenticity of sources is crucial to ensure the validity of the intelligence gathered.

Privacy and Ethical Concerns: Although OSINT involves publicly available information, ethical considerations related to privacy and data protection must be taken into account. Respecting individuals' privacy and adhering to ethical standards is essential.

Legal Limitations: While OSINT relies on open sources, there are legal constraints related to data usage, copyright, and intellectual property. Ensuring compliance with legal requirements is important for conducting lawful and ethical OSINT activities.

Open Source Intelligence (OSINT) is a vital component of modern intelligence and investigative practices, leveraging publicly available information to provide valuable insights and support decision-making. By understanding the OSINT process, its applications, and the challenges involved, professionals can effectively utilize open-source data to achieve their objectives and enhance their operations across various fields.

1.3. The Synergy Between AI and OSINT

The integration of Artificial Intelligence (AI) and Open Source Intelligence (OSINT) represents a transformative shift in how information is collected, analyzed, and utilized. The synergy between AI and OSINT enhances the capabilities of both fields, leveraging AI's computational power and learning algorithms to maximize the effectiveness of OSINT. This chapter explores how AI complements and amplifies OSINT processes, the benefits of their integration, and the impact on various applications.

AI's Enhancement of OSINT Capabilities

Data Collection and Aggregation

One of the primary challenges in OSINT is the vast amount of data available across diverse sources. AI technologies, particularly machine learning and natural language processing (NLP), can automate the collection and aggregation of information from a multitude of open sources. AI-driven tools can crawl websites, scrape social media platforms, and extract relevant data from news articles, blogs, and forums. This automation significantly reduces the time and effort required for data collection, allowing analysts to focus on more strategic tasks.

Web Scraping and Crawling: AI-powered web crawlers can efficiently navigate and extract information from websites, even those with dynamic content. These tools can be programmed to target specific keywords or topics, ensuring that relevant data is captured from various online sources.

Social Media Monitoring: AI algorithms can analyze social media platforms to track mentions, sentiment, and trends. By using NLP techniques, AI can process and understand the context of social media posts, helping analysts to identify emerging issues and public sentiment.

Data Analysis and Pattern Recognition

Once data is collected, the next challenge is to analyze and interpret it effectively. AI enhances this process through advanced analytical techniques that can uncover patterns, correlations, and anomalies within large datasets. Machine learning models can identify trends and insights that might be missed by traditional analysis methods.

Pattern Recognition: AI algorithms can detect patterns and trends in data that may indicate potential threats or opportunities. For example, anomaly detection algorithms can identify unusual behavior or deviations from normal patterns, which can be crucial for spotting security threats or market shifts.

Sentiment Analysis: NLP tools can analyze textual data to determine sentiment and emotional tone. This can be particularly useful for understanding public opinion, assessing brand reputation, and monitoring reactions to events.

Real-Time Analysis and Decision Support

AI's ability to process and analyze data in real-time significantly enhances OSINT's effectiveness in dynamic environments. Real-time analysis allows for the immediate identification of emerging threats, trends, and opportunities.

Real-Time Threat Detection: AI systems can continuously monitor open sources for signs of new threats or suspicious activities. By analyzing data in real-time, these systems can alert analysts to potential issues before they escalate.

Decision Support Systems: AI can support decision-making by providing actionable insights and recommendations based on the analyzed data. This can include automated risk assessments, strategic recommendations, and predictive analytics to guide decision-makers.

Benefits of the AI-OSINT Synergy

Increased Efficiency and Speed

The combination of AI and OSINT drastically increases the efficiency and speed of intelligence operations. AI automates time-consuming tasks such as data collection and analysis, allowing analysts to process larger volumes of data more quickly. This enables faster response times and more agile decision-making.

Enhanced Accuracy and Precision

AI enhances the accuracy and precision of OSINT by minimizing human error and bias. Machine learning models can analyze data with a high degree of accuracy and consistency, providing more reliable and precise insights. AI's ability to process complex datasets and identify subtle patterns improves the overall quality of intelligence.

Scalability

AI-powered OSINT tools can scale to handle large and diverse datasets, making them suitable for applications that require extensive data analysis. Whether monitoring global social media trends or analyzing vast amounts of public records, AI can adapt to varying scales of operation.

Advanced Analytical Capabilities

AI introduces advanced analytical capabilities that go beyond traditional methods. Techniques such as predictive analytics, clustering, and deep learning enable more sophisticated analysis and deeper insights into complex datasets. This advanced analysis helps uncover hidden relationships and trends that might not be apparent through conventional analysis.

Applications of AI-Enhanced OSINT

Cybersecurity

In cybersecurity, AI-enhanced OSINT can be used to monitor for potential threats, analyze cyber attack patterns, and identify vulnerabilities. AI-driven tools can track hacker activities, detect phishing attempts, and analyze malware trends, providing valuable intelligence for protecting digital assets.

Law Enforcement

AI-powered OSINT tools assist law enforcement agencies in tracking criminal activities, monitoring online communities, and gathering evidence. AI can analyze social media posts, detect suspicious behavior, and provide insights into criminal networks and activities.

Market Intelligence

Businesses use AI-enhanced OSINT to gain insights into market trends, competitor activities, and customer behavior. AI tools can analyze market data, monitor industry news, and track competitor strategies, helping organizations make informed business decisions.

National Security

For national security purposes, AI-enhanced OSINT can provide intelligence on geopolitical events, terrorism, and international relations. AI can analyze open sources from around the world, providing valuable insights into global security issues and emerging threats.

Challenges and Considerations

Despite the numerous benefits, integrating AI with OSINT also presents challenges:

Data Privacy and Ethics

The use of AI for OSINT raises concerns about data privacy and ethics. Ensuring that AI tools comply with legal and ethical standards while collecting and analyzing public data is essential to maintain trust and integrity.

Data Quality and Reliability

AI's effectiveness depends on the quality and reliability of the data it processes. Ensuring that the data collected through OSINT is accurate and credible is crucial for producing reliable insights.

Bias and Fairness

AI algorithms can inadvertently introduce bias into the analysis process. It is important to address and mitigate potential biases to ensure fair and unbiased intelligence outcomes.

The synergy between Artificial Intelligence (AI) and Open Source Intelligence (OSINT) represents a powerful fusion of technology and information gathering. By leveraging AI's capabilities to automate, analyze, and enhance OSINT processes, organizations can achieve greater efficiency, accuracy, and depth in their intelligence efforts. The integration of AI and OSINT opens up new possibilities for addressing complex challenges and provides valuable insights across various domains, from cybersecurity to market intelligence. As AI continues to advance, its role in enhancing OSINT will likely become even more significant, shaping the future of intelligence and decision-making.

1.4. The Growing Importance of Cyber Investigations

The significance of cyber investigations has surged dramatically in recent years due to the increasing prevalence and sophistication of cyber threats. As our reliance on digital technologies and online platforms grows, so does the need for effective cyber investigation techniques to protect sensitive information, maintain operational integrity, and uphold security in various sectors. This chapter explores why cyber investigations are becoming increasingly crucial, the driving factors behind this trend, and the implications for organizations and individuals alike.

The Rise of Cyber Threats

Increased Frequency and Sophistication of Attacks

Cyber threats have evolved from simple viruses and malware to highly sophisticated attacks involving advanced persistent threats (APTs), ransomware, and state-sponsored cyber espionage. These threats target individuals, businesses, and government entities, exploiting vulnerabilities in systems and networks to steal data, disrupt operations, or cause financial damage. The growing complexity of cyber attacks necessitates more advanced and comprehensive investigative techniques to effectively detect, respond to, and mitigate these threats.

Expansion of Digital Infrastructure

The expansion of digital infrastructure, including cloud computing, IoT devices, and mobile technologies, has broadened the attack surface for cyber threats. As organizations and individuals increasingly rely on interconnected systems and online platforms, the potential entry points for cybercriminals have multiplied. This proliferation of digital assets and data underscores the need for robust cyber investigations to safeguard against security breaches and data leaks.

Rise in Cybercrime and Cyber Espionage

Cybercrime has become a lucrative enterprise, with criminal organizations and individuals exploiting digital technologies for financial gain. Cybercrime includes activities such as identity theft, financial fraud, and intellectual property theft. Additionally, cyber espionage, often perpetrated by nation-states or politically motivated groups, targets sensitive information for strategic advantage. The growing prevalence of these activities highlights the importance of cyber investigations in identifying perpetrators and preventing further harm.

Implications for Organizations

Protecting Sensitive Information

Organizations are entrusted with vast amounts of sensitive information, including personal data, financial records, and proprietary business information. Cyber investigations play a critical role in protecting this information from unauthorized access, theft, or compromise. Effective investigations help organizations identify vulnerabilities, respond to incidents, and implement measures to prevent future breaches.

Maintaining Operational Integrity

Cyber attacks can disrupt business operations, leading to downtime, loss of productivity, and damage to reputation. Investigating cyber incidents helps organizations understand the impact of attacks, recover from disruptions, and restore normal operations. Timely and effective cyber investigations minimize the operational impact of attacks and support business continuity.

Regulatory Compliance

Regulatory requirements for data protection and cybersecurity are becoming increasingly stringent. Organizations must comply with regulations such as the GDPR, CCPA, and various industry-specific standards. Cyber investigations assist organizations in meeting compliance requirements by providing evidence of data breaches, demonstrating response efforts, and ensuring that regulatory obligations are met.

Risk Management and Prevention

Proactive cyber investigations contribute to effective risk management by identifying potential threats, assessing vulnerabilities, and implementing preventive measures. Investigations help organizations understand emerging threat trends, improve security posture, and develop strategies to mitigate risks before they materialize.

Implications for Individuals

Personal Data Protection

For individuals, cyber investigations are crucial in protecting personal data from theft and misuse. Identity theft, phishing scams, and online fraud can have significant consequences for individuals, including financial loss and reputational damage. Investigations into these incidents help individuals recover stolen data, identify perpetrators, and take preventive actions to safeguard their personal information.

Awareness and Education

The increasing importance of cyber investigations underscores the need for greater awareness and education regarding cybersecurity. Individuals must be informed about common cyber threats, best practices for online safety, and the importance of reporting suspicious activities. Cyber investigations play a role in raising awareness and educating individuals about potential risks and preventive measures.

Legal and Financial Recourse

When individuals fall victim to cybercrime, they may seek legal and financial recourse to recover losses and seek justice. Cyber investigations provide evidence needed for legal actions, insurance claims, and other forms of recourse. Investigators work to uncover the details of the crime, identify perpetrators, and support victims in their pursuit of compensation and resolution.

The Role of Technology in Cyber Investigations

Advanced Tools and Techniques

The growing complexity of cyber threats requires advanced tools and techniques for effective investigations. Technologies such as digital forensics, threat intelligence platforms, and machine learning algorithms enhance investigators' ability to analyze data, detect anomalies, and trace cybercriminal activities. The integration of AI with OSINT, for example, provides powerful capabilities for identifying patterns and extracting actionable insights from vast amounts of data.

Collaboration and Information Sharing

Cyber investigations often involve collaboration between various stakeholders, including law enforcement agencies, private sector organizations, and international partners. Information sharing and collaboration are essential for building comprehensive threat intelligence, coordinating responses, and addressing cross-border cybercrime. Effective cyber investigations rely on a collaborative approach to leverage collective expertise and resources.

Emerging Trends and Future Directions

As technology continues to evolve, so will the nature of cyber threats and investigations. Emerging trends such as quantum computing, blockchain technology, and advanced encryption methods will shape the future of cyber investigations. Staying abreast of these trends and adapting investigative techniques will be crucial for addressing new challenges and ensuring ongoing effectiveness in cyber investigations.

The growing importance of cyber investigations is a reflection of the increasing complexity and prevalence of cyber threats. As digital technologies and online platforms become integral to our lives and businesses, the need for effective cyber investigations to protect sensitive information, maintain operational integrity, and uphold security has never been greater. By leveraging advanced technologies, fostering collaboration, and staying informed about emerging trends, cyber investigations will continue to play a pivotal role in safeguarding against the evolving landscape of cyber threats.

1.5. Objectives and Scope of the Book

This book, "AI and OSINT: The Future of Cyber Investigation," aims to provide a comprehensive exploration of how Artificial Intelligence (AI) and Open Source Intelligence (OSINT) intersect to revolutionize the field of cyber investigation. The objectives and scope of this book are designed to equip readers with the knowledge and tools necessary to harness the synergy between AI and OSINT effectively. This section outlines the key objectives and defines the scope of the book to ensure a clear understanding of what readers can expect.

Objectives of the Book

To Explain the Fundamentals of AI and OSINT

The book seeks to provide a foundational understanding of both Artificial Intelligence and Open Source Intelligence. It covers essential concepts, definitions, and the underlying principles of these fields, ensuring that readers have a solid grasp of the basic concepts before delving into their integration. This objective sets the stage for a deeper exploration of how AI enhances OSINT processes.

To Explore the Integration of AI and OSINT

A primary objective of this book is to explore the synergy between AI and OSINT. It examines how AI technologies, such as machine learning, natural language processing, and computer vision, are applied to OSINT to enhance data collection, analysis, and decision-making. By highlighting the benefits and practical applications of this integration, the book aims to illustrate how AI can transform OSINT practices.

To Provide Practical Insights and Tools

The book aims to offer practical insights and tools for implementing AI-powered OSINT solutions. It includes detailed discussions on AI techniques, OSINT tools, and real-world applications. Readers will gain knowledge about the latest technologies, best practices, and strategies for leveraging AI in OSINT operations. This objective ensures that readers can apply theoretical concepts to practical scenarios.

To Address Challenges and Considerations

Understanding the challenges and ethical considerations associated with AI and OSINT is crucial. This book addresses various challenges, including data privacy, ethical implications, and legal frameworks. It provides guidance on navigating these issues and offers strategies for mitigating potential risks. By addressing these concerns, the book aims to promote responsible and effective use of AI and OSINT.

To Analyze Future Trends and Developments

The book explores future trends and developments in AI and OSINT, providing readers with insights into emerging technologies and evolving practices. It aims to prepare readers for the future landscape of cyber investigation, highlighting potential advancements and their implications for the field. This objective ensures that readers are informed about upcoming changes and can adapt to new developments.

Scope of the Book

Foundational Concepts

The book begins with an introduction to the fundamental concepts of AI and OSINT. It covers the definitions, core components, and historical evolution of both fields. This section sets the groundwork for understanding how AI and OSINT interact and contributes to the overall context of the book.

AI Techniques and Tools

The book delves into various AI techniques and tools that are relevant to OSINT. This includes an exploration of machine learning algorithms, natural language processing, and computer vision technologies. It also covers AI-driven OSINT tools and platforms that facilitate data collection, analysis, and visualization.

Real-World Applications

Practical applications of AI and OSINT are a significant focus of the book. It examines case studies and real-world scenarios where AI-enhanced OSINT has been successfully implemented. This section provides concrete examples of how AI and OSINT are used in cybersecurity, law enforcement, market intelligence, and other domains.

Ethical and Legal Considerations

Ethical and legal considerations are critical when working with AI and OSINT. The book addresses issues related to data privacy, ethical use of technology, and compliance with legal frameworks. It provides guidance on maintaining ethical standards and navigating legal requirements in the context of AI and OSINT.

Future Trends and Innovations

The book explores future trends and innovations in AI and OSINT. It discusses emerging technologies, such as quantum computing and blockchain, and their potential impact on cyber investigation. This section helps readers anticipate future developments and prepare for the evolving landscape of AI and OSINT.

Implementation Challenges

Challenges related to the implementation of AI-powered OSINT solutions are addressed. The book provides insights into common obstacles, such as data quality, system integration, and resource management. It offers practical advice on overcoming these challenges and ensuring successful implementation.

Educational and Professional Development

The book includes resources for further education and professional development in AI and OSINT. It provides recommendations for additional readings, training programs, and professional organizations that can help readers deepen their knowledge and skills in these fields.

The objectives and scope of "AI and OSINT: The Future of Cyber Investigation" are designed to offer a comprehensive and practical exploration of how AI and OSINT intersect to enhance cyber investigations. By covering foundational concepts, practical applications, ethical considerations, and future trends, the book aims to provide readers with a well-rounded understanding of the subject. It equips readers with the knowledge and tools needed to leverage AI in OSINT effectively, addressing both current practices and future developments in the field.

Chapter 2: The Evolution of OSINT in Cybersecurity

Chapter 2, "The Evolution of OSINT in Cybersecurity," takes readers on a journey through the historical development of Open Source Intelligence (OSINT) and its critical role in the cybersecurity landscape. This chapter explores how OSINT has evolved from basic information gathering techniques to a sophisticated discipline essential for identifying and mitigating cyber threats. By examining the strengths and limitations of traditional OSINT methods, the chapter highlights the growing need for innovation and the role of AI in overcoming these challenges. Understanding the evolution of OSINT provides a foundation for appreciating its current and future impact on cybersecurity.

2.1. A Brief History of OSINT

Open Source Intelligence (OSINT) has evolved significantly over the decades, driven by advancements in technology, shifts in information availability, and growing recognition of the value of publicly accessible data. Understanding the historical development of OSINT provides insight into its current practices and future potential. This section outlines the key milestones and developments that have shaped OSINT into the critical field it is today.

Early Beginnings

Pre-Digital Era

The concept of gathering and analyzing information from open sources is not new. Before the digital age, OSINT primarily involved collecting data from traditional media sources such as newspapers, books, public records, and other printed materials. Intelligence professionals and researchers relied on these sources to gather information about geopolitical events, economic conditions, and social trends.

Public Records and Newspapers: Governments, businesses, and individuals accessed public records and newspapers to gather information about political, economic, and social developments. These sources provided valuable insights, though the process was often labor-intensive and limited by physical access and the availability of information.

World War II and the Birth of Modern OSINT

The term "open source intelligence" and the formalization of OSINT practices began to take shape during World War II. The wartime effort to gather information about enemy activities and intentions led to the establishment of dedicated intelligence units that monitored publicly available information, including enemy propaganda and media reports.

Strategic Bombing Surveys: Allied forces conducted strategic bombing surveys and analyzed open sources to assess the impact of bombing campaigns and enemy capabilities. These surveys highlighted the importance of analyzing publicly available data to support military strategy and operations.

Propaganda Analysis: Intelligence agencies focused on analyzing enemy propaganda and public statements to gain insights into enemy morale, intentions, and strategies. This early use of OSINT laid the groundwork for future developments in the field.

The Digital Revolution

Advent of the Internet

The advent of the internet in the late 20th century revolutionized OSINT by dramatically expanding the volume and accessibility of publicly available information. The internet provided a new platform for information dissemination and created opportunities for more efficient and comprehensive data collection.

Growth of Online Resources: The proliferation of websites, forums, and online news sources contributed to a vast increase in the amount of publicly available data. OSINT practitioners could access a broader range of sources and gather information more quickly than ever before.

Early Web Crawlers: The development of web crawlers and search engines enabled the automated collection of online data. These tools made it easier to index and retrieve information from the growing number of websites and online resources.

The Rise of Social Media

The emergence of social media platforms in the early 21st century further transformed OSINT by introducing new sources of real-time, user-generated content. Social media became a critical source of information for tracking public sentiment, monitoring events, and identifying emerging trends.

Real-Time Monitoring: Social media platforms such as Twitter, Facebook, and Instagram provided real-time updates on breaking news, protests, and other significant events. OSINT practitioners began leveraging these platforms to gather timely and relevant information.

User-Generated Content: The proliferation of user-generated content on social media offered new insights into public opinion, individual behavior, and social dynamics. Analyzing this content became an important aspect of OSINT, particularly for understanding trends and sentiments.

Formalization and Professionalization

Establishment of OSINT Communities

As OSINT gained recognition for its value in intelligence and research, dedicated communities and professional organizations emerged to support and advance the field. These communities provided resources, training, and best practices for OSINT practitioners.

OSINT Conferences and Workshops: Conferences and workshops focused on OSINT allowed practitioners to share knowledge, discuss emerging trends, and showcase new tools and techniques. These events facilitated collaboration and innovation within the OSINT community.

Professional Organizations: Organizations such as the Open Source Intelligence Forum (OSIF) and the International OSINT Foundation (IOF) played a key role in promoting OSINT as a discipline and providing resources for professionals in the field.

Integration with Other Intelligence Disciplines

OSINT began to be integrated with other intelligence disciplines, such as signals intelligence (SIGINT) and human intelligence (HUMINT), to provide a more comprehensive understanding of complex issues. This integration enhanced the ability to cross-reference and corroborate information from multiple sources.

Multidisciplinary Approach: Combining OSINT with SIGINT, HUMINT, and other intelligence disciplines allowed for a more holistic approach to intelligence gathering and analysis. This multidisciplinary approach improved the accuracy and reliability of intelligence assessments.

Advanced Analytical Techniques: The integration of OSINT with advanced analytical techniques, such as data mining and machine learning, further enhanced the ability to process and analyze large volumes of data. These techniques enabled more sophisticated analysis and insights.

Current Trends and Future Directions

AI and Automation

The integration of Artificial Intelligence (AI) and automation with OSINT is a current trend that is reshaping the field. AI technologies, such as machine learning and natural language processing, are being used to enhance data collection, analysis, and decision-making.

AI-Powered Tools: AI-powered OSINT tools are capable of processing vast amounts of data, identifying patterns, and generating actionable insights. These tools are improving the efficiency and effectiveness of OSINT operations.

Automation of Routine Tasks: Automation is streamlining routine tasks such as data collection and aggregation, allowing analysts to focus on higher-level analysis and strategic decision-making.

Big Data and Analytics

The growth of big data and advanced analytics is driving innovations in OSINT. The ability to analyze large and diverse datasets is providing new opportunities for intelligence gathering and analysis.

Big Data Technologies: Technologies such as Hadoop and Apache Spark are being used to handle and analyze large volumes of data. These technologies are enabling more effective processing and analysis of big data in OSINT.

Advanced Visualization: Data visualization tools are helping to present complex information in a more accessible and actionable format. Visualizations such as heat maps, graphs, and network diagrams are enhancing the interpretability of OSINT data.

The history of Open Source Intelligence (OSINT) reflects the evolving nature of information gathering and analysis, from early manual methods to the sophisticated, technology-driven practices of today. The field has grown in scope and complexity, driven by advancements in technology, the proliferation of digital and social media, and the increasing recognition of the value of publicly available data. Understanding this historical evolution provides valuable context for appreciating the current state of OSINT and anticipating future developments.

2.2. The Role of OSINT in Early Cybersecurity Efforts

Open Source Intelligence (OSINT) has played a significant role in the evolution of cybersecurity, particularly in its early stages. Before the advent of sophisticated security technologies and advanced threat detection systems, OSINT provided critical insights and support for cybersecurity efforts. This section explores how OSINT contributed to early cybersecurity practices, the challenges faced, and the impact it had on shaping modern cybersecurity strategies.

Initial Cybersecurity Landscape

Early Threat Landscape

In the early days of cybersecurity, threats were relatively simple compared to today's sophisticated attacks. Cybersecurity efforts primarily focused on protecting systems from basic forms of malware, unauthorized access, and simple network attacks. The early threat landscape was characterized by relatively straightforward attack vectors and limited awareness of cybersecurity best practices.

Malware and Viruses: The primary threats included viruses, worms, and basic forms of malware that could disrupt system operations and compromise data. Early cybersecurity efforts concentrated on detecting and mitigating these threats.

Unauthorized Access: Protecting against unauthorized access and ensuring the integrity of systems and networks were key concerns. Early cybersecurity measures focused on implementing basic access controls and authentication mechanisms.

Role of OSINT in Early Cybersecurity

Even in the nascent stages of cybersecurity, OSINT played a crucial role in gathering information about potential threats and vulnerabilities. OSINT methods included monitoring publicly available information sources to identify emerging threats and understanding the broader context of cybersecurity issues.

Public Disclosures and Bulletins: OSINT involved monitoring public disclosures, security bulletins, and advisories issued by organizations such as CERT (Computer Emergency Response Team) and vendor-specific security teams. These sources provided valuable information about vulnerabilities, patches, and emerging threats.

Security Research and Publications: Early cybersecurity research, white papers, and academic publications were critical OSINT sources. Researchers and analysts used these publications to stay informed about new threats, attack methods, and defensive strategies.

Early OSINT Techniques and Tools

Manual Data Collection

Before the development of advanced OSINT tools, cybersecurity professionals relied on manual methods to collect and analyze data. This involved searching through public forums, news articles, and technical documentation to gather relevant information.

Online Forums and Newsgroups: Early cybersecurity communities and forums, such as Usenet groups and specialized mailing lists, were valuable sources of information. Security professionals and researchers shared insights, vulnerabilities, and attack methods in these forums.

Technical Documentation: Technical manuals, product documentation, and security advisories were key sources of information for understanding vulnerabilities and security configurations. OSINT practitioners used these documents to stay updated on security best practices and emerging threats.

Early Detection Systems

Early OSINT techniques also included the development and use of basic detection systems that relied on publicly available information. These systems were designed to identify potential threats and vulnerabilities based on known patterns and signatures.

Signature-Based Detection: Early detection systems used signature-based methods to identify known malware and attack patterns. OSINT data, such as known virus signatures and attack vectors, was used to create and update these signatures.

Vulnerability Databases: Vulnerability databases, such as the National Vulnerability Database (NVD), provided information about known vulnerabilities and their associated risks. Early OSINT efforts involved leveraging these databases to identify and address vulnerabilities in systems.

Challenges in Early OSINT for Cybersecurity

Limited Information Sources

In the early days of OSINT, information sources were limited compared to today's vast array of online resources. The scope of publicly available information was narrower, and gathering relevant data required significant manual effort.

Data Scarcity: Early cybersecurity professionals faced challenges in finding comprehensive and timely information about emerging threats and vulnerabilities. The lack of centralized information sources made it difficult to stay updated on the latest developments.

Information Fragmentation: Information about threats and vulnerabilities was often fragmented across various sources. Analysts had to piece together information from disparate sources to form a complete picture of the threat landscape.

Lack of Advanced Tools

The absence of advanced OSINT tools and technologies meant that early cybersecurity efforts relied heavily on manual analysis and traditional methods. This limited the ability to process and analyze large volumes of data efficiently.

Manual Analysis: Early OSINT analysis involved manually reviewing and interpreting data from various sources. This process was time-consuming and prone to errors, making it challenging to keep up with rapidly evolving threats.

Limited Automation: Automation tools for data collection, analysis, and threat detection were not widely available. This limited the ability to scale OSINT efforts and respond quickly to emerging threats.

Impact of Early OSINT on Modern Cybersecurity

Foundation for Modern Practices

Early OSINT practices laid the groundwork for modern cybersecurity strategies and tools. The lessons learned from early OSINT efforts helped shape the development of advanced threat detection systems, automated tools, and comprehensive cybersecurity frameworks.

Advancements in Threat Intelligence: The early use of OSINT highlighted the importance of threat intelligence in cybersecurity. Modern threat intelligence platforms build on these early practices by incorporating advanced data collection, analysis, and automation techniques.

Integration with Other Disciplines: Early OSINT practices demonstrated the value of integrating publicly available information with other cybersecurity disciplines, such as intrusion detection and incident response. Modern cybersecurity approaches continue to leverage this integration to enhance overall security posture.

Evolution of OSINT Tools and Techniques

The evolution of OSINT tools and techniques has significantly enhanced cybersecurity efforts. Advances in technology, including AI and machine learning, have transformed OSINT into a powerful tool for threat detection, analysis, and response.

Automated OSINT Tools: Modern OSINT tools automate data collection, analysis, and visualization, enabling faster and more comprehensive threat assessments. These tools leverage advanced algorithms and machine learning to process large volumes of data and identify patterns.

Enhanced Data Sources: The proliferation of digital and social media has expanded the range of OSINT sources available to cybersecurity professionals. This expanded data landscape provides richer insights into emerging threats and vulnerabilities.

The role of OSINT in early cybersecurity efforts was instrumental in shaping the field and laying the foundation for modern practices. Despite the challenges of limited information sources and manual analysis, early OSINT practices provided valuable insights and support for cybersecurity efforts. The evolution of OSINT tools and techniques has significantly enhanced the ability to detect, analyze, and respond to threats, contributing to the development of more sophisticated and effective cybersecurity strategies. Understanding the historical context of OSINT in cybersecurity provides valuable insights into its current and future applications in protecting digital assets and maintaining security.

2.3. Traditional OSINT Techniques: Strengths and Weaknesses

Open Source Intelligence (OSINT) has been a crucial component of information gathering and analysis for many years. Traditional OSINT techniques, employed before the advent of advanced digital tools, have laid the groundwork for modern practices. Understanding these techniques' strengths and weaknesses provides valuable context for appreciating their role in intelligence gathering and how they have evolved over time.

Traditional OSINT Techniques

Manual Data Collection

Manual data collection involves gathering information from various open sources through physical or digital means. This method includes reviewing newspapers, public records, and academic journals, as well as searching through online forums and bulletin boards.

Strengths:

- **Richness of Data**: Manual collection allows analysts to access a broad range of sources, including niche publications and local news, which can provide unique insights not available through automated systems.
- **Contextual Understanding**: Analysts can interpret the context and relevance of information more effectively when manually reviewing sources. This helps in understanding nuances and subtleties in the data.

Weaknesses:

- **Time-Consuming**: Manual data collection is labor-intensive and time-consuming. Analysts must sift through large volumes of information, which can delay the timely acquisition of relevant data.
- **Inconsistency**: The quality and relevance of data can vary, leading to inconsistencies in the collected information. Analysts may also encounter difficulties in verifying the credibility of sources.

Public Records and Reports

Accessing public records and reports involves retrieving information from government databases, regulatory filings, and official reports. These sources include financial disclosures, legal documents, and governmental announcements.

Strengths:

- **Credibility**: Public records and official reports are often considered reliable and authoritative sources of information. They provide verifiable data and are usually subject to regulatory standards.
- **Structured Information**: These sources typically present information in a structured format, making it easier to analyze and extract relevant details.

Weaknesses:

- **Limited Scope**: Public records may not cover all aspects of a particular subject, leading to gaps in the information. Additionally, some records may be outdated or incomplete.
- **Accessibility Issues**: Accessing certain public records may involve bureaucratic hurdles or restrictions, making it challenging to obtain the necessary information in a timely manner.

Traditional Media Monitoring

Monitoring traditional media involves analyzing content from newspapers, television broadcasts, radio programs, and magazines. This technique includes tracking news stories, editorials, and feature articles relevant to the subject of interest.

Strengths:

- **Timeliness**: Traditional media often provides timely updates on current events and developments. This immediacy is valuable for tracking unfolding situations and obtaining up-to-date information.
- **Diverse Perspectives**: Media sources offer diverse viewpoints and opinions, which can provide a well-rounded understanding of events and issues.

Weaknesses:

- **Bias and Accuracy**: Media reports may be subject to bias, inaccuracies, or sensationalism. Analysts must critically evaluate the credibility and objectivity of media sources.

- **Information Overload**: The sheer volume of media content can lead to information overload, making it difficult to identify and extract relevant details efficiently.

Interviews and Human Sources

Conducting interviews with individuals and utilizing human sources involves gathering information through direct communication with people who have relevant knowledge or expertise. This technique includes formal interviews, informal conversations, and expert consultations.

Strengths:

- **Insightful Information**: Interviews and human sources can provide valuable insights and firsthand accounts that may not be available through other methods. This technique allows for probing deeper into specific topics and obtaining nuanced information.
- **Verification**: Direct interactions with sources can help verify the authenticity of information and clarify ambiguities.

Weaknesses:

- **Subjectivity**: Information obtained from interviews and human sources may be subjective and influenced by the source's perspectives or biases. Analysts must critically assess the reliability and motives of the sources.
- **Time and Resource Intensive**: Conducting interviews and managing human sources requires significant time and resources. This technique may also involve logistical challenges, such as coordinating schedules and ensuring confidentiality.

Library and Archival Research

Library and archival research involves accessing historical documents, research papers, and archival materials. This technique includes reviewing academic studies, historical records, and institutional archives to gather background information and context.

Strengths:

- **Historical Context**: Library and archival research provides valuable historical context and background information that can enhance understanding of current issues and trends.
- **Depth of Information**: These sources often contain in-depth analyses, detailed records, and comprehensive data that contribute to a thorough investigation.

Weaknesses:

- **Limited Relevance**: Historical and archival sources may not always be directly relevant to current issues, leading to potential gaps in the information. Additionally, accessing certain archives may be restricted or require special permissions.
- **Static Nature**: Unlike real-time sources, library and archival materials may not provide the most up-to-date information, potentially limiting their usefulness for tracking ongoing developments.

Evolution and Adaptation

Traditional OSINT techniques have laid a solid foundation for modern intelligence practices. However, the field has evolved significantly with the advent of digital technologies and advanced analytical tools. Modern OSINT now incorporates automated data collection, real-time monitoring, and sophisticated analytics, addressing many of the limitations of traditional methods.

Integration with Digital Tools: The integration of digital tools and technologies has enhanced the efficiency and effectiveness of OSINT. Automated systems can process vast amounts of data, identify patterns, and provide real-time insights, overcoming some of the challenges associated with manual methods.

Expanded Data Sources: The availability of digital and social media platforms has expanded the range of data sources, providing richer and more diverse information. This expansion allows for more comprehensive and timely intelligence gathering.

Traditional OSINT techniques have played a crucial role in intelligence gathering, each with its strengths and weaknesses. While manual data collection, public records, media monitoring, interviews, and archival research have provided valuable insights, they also faced challenges related to time, scope, and accuracy. The evolution of OSINT, driven by advancements in technology, has addressed many of these challenges, leading to more efficient and effective intelligence practices. Understanding the historical context and limitations of traditional OSINT techniques provides valuable insights into the development of modern OSINT practices and their continued importance in the field of intelligence and cybersecurity.

2.4. The Rise of Digital Footprints and Big Data

The emergence of digital footprints and the growth of big data have profoundly transformed the landscape of Open Source Intelligence (OSINT). This section explores how digital footprints and big data have reshaped intelligence gathering, the opportunities and challenges they present, and their impact on modern OSINT practices.

Digital Footprints

Definition and Evolution

Digital footprints refer to the trail of data that individuals leave behind as they interact with digital platforms and services. This data can include social media activity, online purchases, website visits, and other forms of digital engagement. The rise of the internet, mobile devices, and social media has significantly expanded the scope and volume of digital footprints.

Early Digital Footprints: In the early days of the internet, digital footprints were relatively simple, primarily consisting of email communications and basic website interactions. As technology evolved, the complexity and volume of digital footprints increased.

Modern Digital Footprints: Today, digital footprints encompass a wide range of data, including social media posts, geolocation data, online shopping behavior, and interactions with various digital platforms. This data provides a comprehensive view of an individual's online presence and activities.

Opportunities for OSINT

Digital footprints offer valuable opportunities for OSINT by providing insights into individuals' behaviors, preferences, and affiliations. This data can be used for various purposes, including threat assessment, background checks, and sentiment analysis.

Behavioral Analysis: Analyzing digital footprints allows OSINT practitioners to understand individuals' online behaviors and preferences. This information can be used to identify patterns, predict actions, and assess potential risks.

Social Media Monitoring: Social media platforms are rich sources of digital footprints. Monitoring social media activity provides real-time insights into public sentiment, trends, and emerging issues. This can be valuable for tracking public reactions to events, identifying influencers, and detecting potential threats.

Challenges and Privacy Concerns

The proliferation of digital footprints raises challenges related to privacy, data security, and ethical considerations. Ensuring responsible and ethical use of digital data is essential for maintaining trust and compliance with legal standards.

Privacy Issues: The extensive collection and analysis of digital footprints can raise privacy concerns. Individuals may be unaware of the extent to which their data is being collected and analyzed, leading to potential privacy violations.

Data Security: Ensuring the security of digital data is crucial to prevent unauthorized access and misuse. Organizations must implement robust data protection measures to safeguard sensitive information.

Big Data

Definition and Characteristics

Big data refers to extremely large and complex datasets that are beyond the capability of traditional data processing tools to manage and analyze. Big data is characterized by its volume, variety, velocity, and veracity.

Volume: The sheer amount of data generated from various sources, including social media, sensors, and transactional systems, contributes to the volume of big data.

Variety: Big data encompasses diverse types of data, including structured data (e.g., databases), unstructured data (e.g., text, images), and semi-structured data (e.g., JSON files).

Velocity: The speed at which data is generated and processed is a key characteristic of big data. Real-time data streams require rapid processing and analysis.

Veracity: Ensuring the accuracy and reliability of big data is crucial for generating meaningful insights. Veracity addresses the quality and trustworthiness of the data.

Impact on OSINT

The rise of big data has significantly impacted OSINT by providing a vast amount of information for analysis. Big data analytics tools and techniques enable OSINT practitioners to process and extract insights from large and diverse datasets.

Enhanced Data Analysis: Big data analytics tools, such as Hadoop and Apache Spark, allow for the processing of large datasets, enabling more comprehensive and detailed analysis. These tools can identify patterns, correlations, and trends that may not be apparent from smaller datasets.

Real-Time Insights: The ability to process and analyze data in real time enhances the timeliness and relevance of OSINT. Real-time analysis enables quick responses to emerging threats, trends, and incidents.

Challenges and Considerations

While big data offers significant opportunities for OSINT, it also presents challenges related to data management, analysis, and interpretation.

Data Management: Managing and storing large volumes of data can be complex and resource-intensive. Organizations must invest in infrastructure and technologies to handle big data effectively.

Complexity of Analysis: Analyzing big data requires advanced analytical techniques and tools. The complexity of processing diverse data types and extracting actionable insights can be a challenge.

Ethical and Legal Concerns: The use of big data in OSINT must comply with ethical and legal standards. Ensuring transparency, consent, and data protection is essential to address concerns related to privacy and data security.

Integration of Digital Footprints and Big Data in OSINT

Comprehensive Intelligence Gathering

Integrating digital footprints and big data enhances OSINT by providing a more comprehensive view of individuals, organizations, and events. The combination of digital footprints and big data analytics enables a more detailed and accurate assessment of potential threats and opportunities.

Cross-Referencing Data: OSINT practitioners can cross-reference digital footprints with big data to validate information and identify inconsistencies. This cross-referencing enhances the reliability of intelligence findings.

Predictive Analysis: Leveraging big data analytics allows for predictive analysis, helping to anticipate future trends and behaviors based on historical data and patterns. This capability is valuable for proactive threat detection and risk assessment.

Enhanced Visualization and Reporting

Advanced data visualization tools help present complex big data insights in an accessible and actionable format. Visualization techniques, such as heat maps, network diagrams, and trend graphs, facilitate the interpretation and communication of intelligence findings.

Visualization Tools: Tools like Tableau and Power BI enable the creation of interactive dashboards and visualizations that make it easier to identify trends, patterns, and anomalies in big data.

Reporting and Communication: Effective reporting and communication of intelligence findings are crucial for decision-making. Visualization enhances the clarity and impact of intelligence reports, making it easier for stakeholders to understand and act on the information.

The rise of digital footprints and big data has revolutionized the field of Open Source Intelligence (OSINT), offering new opportunities for comprehensive and real-time intelligence gathering. While digital footprints provide valuable insights into individual behaviors and preferences, big data analytics enable the processing and analysis of large and diverse datasets. The integration of these elements enhances OSINT capabilities, providing more detailed and accurate intelligence. However, the use of digital footprints and big data also presents challenges related to privacy, data management, and ethical considerations. Understanding the impact of these developments is essential for effectively leveraging OSINT in the modern digital landscape.

2.5. The Necessity of AI in Modern OSINT Practices

The integration of Artificial Intelligence (AI) into Open Source Intelligence (OSINT) practices has become increasingly essential as the volume, complexity, and speed of data continue to grow. AI technologies enhance the ability to collect, process, and analyze vast amounts of open-source data, addressing many of the challenges associated with traditional OSINT methods. This section explores the necessity of AI in modern OSINT, highlighting its contributions to data processing, analysis, and decision-making.

The Expanding Data Landscape

Data Volume and Complexity

The modern digital landscape generates an unprecedented volume of data from diverse sources, including social media, news articles, blogs, forums, and more. This data is often unstructured and heterogeneous, making it challenging to analyze manually.

Volume: The sheer amount of data being generated daily far exceeds human processing capabilities. Manual analysis is impractical for large-scale data sets, requiring automated solutions to manage and extract insights.

Complexity: Data comes in various formats, including text, images, videos, and metadata. The complexity of analyzing such diverse data types necessitates advanced tools capable of handling and integrating multiple forms of information.

Speed of Data Generation

The rapid pace at which data is generated demands real-time processing and analysis. Events and trends can evolve quickly, and timely intelligence is critical for effective decision-making and threat mitigation.

Real-Time Analysis: AI-powered tools can process data in real-time, providing immediate insights into emerging threats and trends. This capability is crucial for responding to fast-moving situations and making informed decisions.

Continuous Monitoring: AI enables continuous monitoring of digital sources, ensuring that intelligence is up-to-date and relevant. This continuous monitoring is essential for tracking ongoing events and detecting changes in patterns.

AI Enhancements in Data Processing

Automated Data Collection

AI technologies automate the collection of data from diverse sources, streamlining the process and increasing efficiency. Automated data collection tools can crawl websites, social media platforms, and other online sources to gather relevant information.

Web Crawlers: AI-powered web crawlers systematically browse the internet to collect data from various sites. These crawlers can be programmed to target specific types of information and update their findings regularly.

Social Media Aggregators: AI tools aggregate data from social media platforms, capturing posts, comments, and interactions. This aggregation provides a comprehensive view of social media activity and sentiment.

Data Cleaning and Preparation

The process of preparing data for analysis involves cleaning, normalizing, and structuring it to ensure accuracy and consistency. AI can automate these tasks, reducing the time and effort required for data preparation.

Data Cleaning: AI algorithms identify and rectify errors, duplicates, and inconsistencies in data. This cleaning process enhances the quality and reliability of the data.

Data Normalization: AI tools standardize data formats and structures, making it easier to integrate and analyze information from different sources. Normalization ensures that data is compatible and usable for analysis.

AI-Driven Data Analysis

Pattern Recognition and Anomaly Detection

AI excels at identifying patterns and anomalies in large datasets. Machine learning algorithms can analyze data to detect unusual behaviors, trends, and potential threats.

Pattern Recognition: AI algorithms recognize patterns in data, such as recurring keywords, behaviors, or connections. This pattern recognition helps identify trends and predict future developments.

Anomaly Detection: AI systems detect anomalies or deviations from expected patterns. Anomaly detection is valuable for identifying unusual activities that may indicate security threats or emerging issues.

Natural Language Processing (NLP)

Natural Language Processing (NLP) enables AI to understand and interpret human language. NLP techniques are crucial for analyzing text data, extracting meaning, and identifying relevant information.

Sentiment Analysis: NLP tools analyze the sentiment of text data, such as social media posts or news articles. Sentiment analysis helps gauge public opinion and emotional responses to events.

Entity Recognition: NLP algorithms identify and classify entities (e.g., people, organizations, locations) mentioned in text. This entity recognition aids in extracting meaningful insights and relationships from textual data.

Predictive Analytics

Predictive analytics uses AI to forecast future trends and outcomes based on historical data. This capability is valuable for anticipating potential risks and opportunities.

Trend Prediction: AI models analyze historical data to identify trends and make predictions about future developments. Predictive analytics helps organizations prepare for upcoming challenges and opportunities.

Risk Assessment: AI-driven risk assessment tools evaluate potential risks based on data patterns and historical trends. This assessment supports proactive decision-making and risk mitigation strategies.

Challenges and Considerations

Data Privacy and Security

The use of AI in OSINT raises concerns about data privacy and security. Ensuring that AI tools comply with privacy regulations and protect sensitive information is essential.

Compliance: AI systems must adhere to privacy laws and regulations, such as GDPR, to protect individuals' personal information. Compliance ensures ethical data handling practices.

Data Protection: Implementing robust security measures to protect data from unauthorized access and breaches is critical. Data protection practices safeguard sensitive information and maintain trust.

Bias and Accuracy

AI systems can exhibit biases based on the data they are trained on. Addressing bias and ensuring the accuracy of AI-driven insights is important for reliable intelligence.

Bias Mitigation: Efforts to identify and mitigate biases in AI algorithms are necessary to ensure fair and unbiased analysis. This includes evaluating training data and algorithmic processes.

Accuracy: Regularly validating and calibrating AI models helps maintain the accuracy and reliability of insights. Accurate data and analysis are crucial for effective decision-making.

The necessity of AI in modern OSINT practices is driven by the expanding volume, complexity, and speed of data. AI technologies enhance data processing, analysis, and decision-making by automating tasks, recognizing patterns, and providing real-time insights. While AI offers significant advantages, it also presents challenges related to data privacy, security, and bias. Embracing AI in OSINT requires a balanced approach that leverages its capabilities while addressing ethical and practical considerations. Understanding the role of AI in OSINT is essential for harnessing its potential and advancing intelligence practices in the digital age.

Chapter 3: AI Techniques for Enhancing OSINT

Chapter 3, "AI Techniques for Enhancing OSINT," delves into the specific Artificial Intelligence (AI) methodologies that are revolutionizing Open Source Intelligence (OSINT). This chapter introduces cutting-edge AI techniques such as machine learning, natural language processing, and image recognition, demonstrating how they are used to automate and enhance the analysis of vast amounts of open-source data. By focusing on these technologies, the chapter illustrates how AI can uncover hidden patterns, detect anomalies, and generate actionable insights more efficiently than ever before. As the backbone of modern OSINT, these AI techniques are essential for staying ahead in the fast-paced world of cyber investigations.

3.1. Machine Learning Algorithms for OSINT

Machine learning (ML) algorithms play a pivotal role in enhancing Open Source Intelligence (OSINT) by automating data analysis, identifying patterns, and generating actionable insights from large and complex datasets. This section explores the various machine learning algorithms that are commonly used in OSINT, their functionalities, and their impact on intelligence gathering.

Types of Machine Learning Algorithms

Supervised Learning Algorithms

Supervised learning algorithms are trained on labeled data, where the input data is paired with known outputs. These algorithms learn to map input features to the correct output, enabling them to make predictions on new, unseen data.

Classification Algorithms:

- **Logistic Regression**: Used for binary classification tasks, such as determining whether a social media post is related to a specific topic or not. It calculates the probability of a categorical outcome based on input features.
- **Support Vector Machines (SVM)**: Effective for classifying data into distinct categories by finding the hyperplane that best separates the classes. SVMs are used for tasks such as sentiment analysis and categorizing content.
- **Decision Trees and Random Forests**: Decision trees split data based on feature values to classify or predict outcomes. Random forests, an ensemble

method, combine multiple decision trees to improve accuracy and robustness. They are used for classifying documents, identifying entities, and detecting anomalies.

Regression Algorithms:

- **Linear Regression**: Used to predict continuous outcomes based on input features. For example, it can forecast trends in data or estimate the likelihood of certain events based on historical data.
- **Polynomial Regression**: Extends linear regression to capture non-linear relationships between variables. It is useful for modeling complex patterns in data.

Unsupervised Learning Algorithms

Unsupervised learning algorithms analyze data without predefined labels or categories. They are used to uncover hidden patterns, group similar data points, and reduce data dimensionality.

Clustering Algorithms:

- **K-Means Clustering**: Groups data points into k clusters based on their similarity. K-means is used for segmenting social media users into groups with similar interests or behaviors.
- **Hierarchical Clustering**: Builds a hierarchy of clusters by either merging smaller clusters (agglomerative) or dividing a large cluster (divisive). It is useful for identifying hierarchical relationships and structures in data.

Dimensionality Reduction Algorithms:

- **Principal Component Analysis (PCA):** Reduces the number of features while preserving the variance in the data. PCA is used to simplify data analysis and visualization by focusing on the most important features.
- **t-Distributed Stochastic Neighbor Embedding (t-SNE):** Projects high-dimensional data into a lower-dimensional space for visualization. t-SNE is useful for exploring and understanding complex data structures.

Semi-Supervised Learning Algorithms

Semi-supervised learning algorithms use a combination of labeled and unlabeled data for training. They leverage the strengths of both supervised and unsupervised learning to improve model performance.

Self-Training: A model trained on labeled data generates pseudo-labels for unlabeled data, which are then used to retrain and refine the model. This approach enhances the model's ability to generalize from limited labeled data.

Co-Training: Utilizes multiple models, each trained on different views or features of the data, to label unlabeled examples. The models then exchange labels to improve each other's performance.

Applications of Machine Learning in OSINT

Text and Sentiment Analysis

Machine learning algorithms are used to analyze textual data from sources such as social media, news articles, and forums. These algorithms extract meaningful information, identify sentiments, and categorize content.

- **Sentiment Analysis**: Classifies the sentiment of text as positive, negative, or neutral. Sentiment analysis helps understand public opinion and emotional responses to events or topics.
- **Named Entity Recognition (NER):** Identifies and classifies entities such as people, organizations, and locations within text. NER is used to extract key information and establish relationships between entities.

Anomaly Detection

Anomaly detection algorithms identify unusual or unexpected patterns in data that may indicate potential threats or anomalies.

- **Fraud Detection**: Machine learning models detect fraudulent activities by identifying deviations from normal patterns in financial transactions or online behaviors.
- **Intrusion Detection**: Identifies unusual network activities that may signify security breaches or cyberattacks. Anomaly detection helps in early detection and response to potential threats.

Predictive Analytics

Predictive analytics uses machine learning algorithms to forecast future events or trends based on historical data. This capability enables proactive decision-making and risk management.

- **Trend Prediction**: Forecasts future trends based on historical data patterns. Predictive analytics helps anticipate market trends, emerging issues, and changes in public sentiment.
- **Risk Assessment**: Evaluates the likelihood of potential risks or threats based on historical data and current patterns. Risk assessment supports strategic planning and threat mitigation.

Image and Video Analysis

Machine learning algorithms are used to analyze images and videos, extracting relevant information and identifying objects or activities.

- **Object Detection**: Identifies and classifies objects within images or video frames. Object detection is used for monitoring surveillance footage or analyzing visual content on social media.
- **Facial Recognition**: Identifies and verifies individuals based on facial features. Facial recognition is used for security, identity verification, and tracking individuals in digital environments.

Challenges and Considerations

Data Quality and Bias

The quality and bias of data used for training machine learning models impact their accuracy and effectiveness. Ensuring high-quality, representative, and unbiased data is essential for reliable results.

- **Data Quality**: Inaccurate, incomplete, or noisy data can lead to misleading insights and incorrect predictions. Data cleaning and preprocessing are crucial for ensuring data quality.
- **Bias**: Machine learning models can inherit biases present in training data. Addressing bias and ensuring fairness in algorithms is important for ethical and accurate analysis.

Scalability and Computational Resources

Machine learning algorithms require significant computational resources, especially when handling large datasets or complex models. Ensuring scalability and efficient resource management is essential for practical implementation.

- **Computational Resources**: Training and deploying machine learning models require substantial processing power and memory. Cloud-based solutions and distributed computing can help manage resource demands.
- **Scalability**: Algorithms must be scalable to handle growing data volumes and increasing complexity. Scalable solutions ensure that models remain effective and responsive to changing data conditions.

Machine learning algorithms are integral to modern Open Source Intelligence (OSINT), enhancing data processing, analysis, and insight generation. By leveraging supervised, unsupervised, and semi-supervised learning techniques, OSINT practitioners can effectively analyze large and complex datasets, detect patterns, and make informed decisions. While machine learning offers significant advantages, challenges related to data quality, bias, and computational resources must be addressed to maximize its effectiveness. Understanding and applying machine learning algorithms in OSINT is essential for harnessing the full potential of AI-driven intelligence in the digital age.

3.2. Natural Language Processing (NLP) for Text and Sentiment Analysis

Natural Language Processing (NLP) is a critical component of modern Open Source Intelligence (OSINT), enabling machines to understand, interpret, and analyze human language. NLP techniques are particularly valuable for text and sentiment analysis, providing insights into large volumes of textual data from various sources, such as social media, news articles, forums, and emails. This section delves into the role of NLP in text and sentiment analysis, exploring key concepts, techniques, and applications.

Introduction to Natural Language Processing (NLP)

NLP is a field of artificial intelligence (AI) focused on the interaction between computers and human language. It encompasses various methods and algorithms designed to process and analyze natural language data, making it possible for computers to understand and generate human-like text.

Core NLP Tasks

- **Tokenization**: The process of breaking down text into smaller units, such as words or phrases, called tokens. Tokenization is a fundamental step in text processing and analysis.
- **Part-of-Speech (POS) Tagging**: Assigning grammatical tags (e.g., noun, verb, adjective) to each token in a text. POS tagging helps in understanding the syntactic structure and meaning of sentences.
- **Named Entity Recognition (NER)**: Identifying and classifying entities such as names, organizations, locations, and dates within a text. NER is used to extract key information and establish relationships between entities.
- **Parsing**: Analyzing the grammatical structure of sentences to understand their meaning and relationships between words. Parsing helps in syntactic and semantic analysis.

Text Analysis with NLP

- Text analysis involves extracting meaningful information from textual data. NLP techniques are employed to analyze text for various purposes, including information retrieval, summarization, and categorization.

Text Classification

- **Topic Classification**: Categorizing text into predefined topics or categories based on its content. This is useful for organizing and managing large volumes of text data, such as news articles or research papers.
- **Spam Detection**: Identifying and filtering out unwanted or irrelevant text, such as spam emails or messages. Machine learning models trained on labeled data can classify text as spam or non-spam.

Information Extraction

- **Entity Extraction**: Identifying and extracting specific entities (e.g., names, dates, locations) from text. This information is used for building knowledge bases and extracting relevant details.
- **Relation Extraction**: Determining relationships between entities mentioned in text. For example, identifying the relationship between people, organizations, and events in news articles.

Text Summarization

- **Extractive Summarization**: Selecting and combining key sentences or phrases from the original text to create a concise summary. Extractive summarization preserves important information while reducing the length of the text.
- **Abstractive Summarization**: Generating new sentences that capture the main ideas of the text, rather than directly extracting portions of it. Abstractive summarization provides more coherent and human-like summaries.

Sentiment Analysis with NLP

Sentiment analysis involves determining the emotional tone or sentiment expressed in a piece of text. It is widely used to gauge public opinion, monitor brand reputation, and assess reactions to events or products.

Sentiment Classification

- **Binary Sentiment Classification**: Categorizing text into two sentiment classes, such as positive or negative. This approach provides a simple overview of the sentiment expressed in the text.
- **Multiclass Sentiment Classification**: Classifying text into multiple sentiment categories, such as positive, negative, neutral, and mixed. Multiclass classification provides a more nuanced understanding of sentiment.

Emotion Detection

Emotion Classification: Identifying specific emotions expressed in text, such as joy, anger, sadness, or fear. Emotion detection helps in understanding the emotional context of the text and its impact on readers.

Aspect-Based Sentiment Analysis

- **Aspect Extraction**: Identifying and extracting specific aspects or features mentioned in the text, such as product features or service attributes. Aspect-based sentiment analysis assesses sentiment related to particular aspects.
- **Aspect Sentiment Analysis**: Evaluating sentiment related to specific aspects identified in the text. This approach provides detailed insights into how different aspects are perceived.

Techniques and Algorithms in NLP

Machine Learning Approaches

- **Naive Bayes Classifier**: A probabilistic classifier based on Bayes' theorem, commonly used for text classification and sentiment analysis. It is simple yet effective for many text analysis tasks.
- **Support Vector Machines (SVM):** A classification algorithm that finds the optimal hyperplane to separate different classes. SVMs are used for text classification and sentiment analysis.
- **Decision Trees and Random Forests**: Decision trees split data based on features to classify or predict outcomes. Random forests combine multiple decision trees to improve accuracy and robustness.

Deep Learning Approaches

- **Recurrent Neural Networks (RNNs):** Neural networks designed for sequential data, such as text. RNNs are used for tasks like text generation and sentiment analysis.
- **Long Short-Term Memory (LSTM) Networks**: A type of RNN that addresses issues with long-term dependencies. LSTMs are effective for understanding context and relationships in text.
- **Transformer Models**: Advanced models such as BERT (Bidirectional Encoder Representations from Transformers) and GPT (Generative Pre-trained Transformer) that leverage attention mechanisms to understand context and meaning in text. These models achieve state-of-the-art performance in various NLP tasks.

Applications in OSINT

Monitoring and Analysis

- **Social Media Monitoring**: Analyzing social media posts and comments to track public sentiment, identify trends, and detect emerging issues. NLP techniques help in filtering and categorizing large volumes of social media data.
- **News and Media Analysis**: Extracting insights from news articles and media reports to monitor events, assess public opinion, and identify potential threats. NLP tools help in summarizing and analyzing media content.

Customer Feedback and Market Research

- **Customer Reviews**: Analyzing customer reviews and feedback to gauge product satisfaction, identify issues, and improve services. Sentiment analysis provides insights into customer experiences and preferences.
- **Market Trends**: Evaluating market trends and consumer sentiment based on textual data from surveys, reviews, and social media. NLP helps in understanding market dynamics and consumer behavior.

Challenges and Considerations

Ambiguity and Context

- **Ambiguity**: Natural language is often ambiguous and context-dependent. NLP models must handle variations in language and context to accurately interpret and analyze text.
- **Context Understanding**: Capturing the context of words and phrases is essential for accurate sentiment analysis and text interpretation. Advanced models like transformers help address context-related challenges.

Data Quality and Bias

- **Data Quality**: High-quality training data is crucial for effective NLP. Inaccurate or biased data can lead to unreliable results and skewed analysis.
- **Bias**: NLP models can inherit biases present in training data. Addressing bias and ensuring fairness in NLP applications is important for ethical and accurate analysis.

Natural Language Processing (NLP) is a powerful tool for text and sentiment analysis in Open Source Intelligence (OSINT). By leveraging NLP techniques, OSINT practitioners can extract valuable insights from large volumes of textual data, monitor public sentiment, and make informed decisions. While NLP offers significant advantages, challenges related to ambiguity, context, and data quality must be addressed to ensure accurate and reliable analysis. Understanding and applying NLP techniques is essential for harnessing the full potential of text and sentiment analysis in the digital age.

3.3. AI in Image and Video Recognition

Artificial Intelligence (AI) has revolutionized image and video recognition, significantly enhancing Open Source Intelligence (OSINT) capabilities. By leveraging advanced algorithms and models, AI can analyze visual data, extract meaningful information, and support a wide range of applications in intelligence gathering, security, and surveillance. This section explores the role of AI in image and video recognition, detailing key techniques, applications, and challenges.

Introduction to Image and Video Recognition

Image and video recognition involves the use of AI to analyze visual content, identify objects, scenes, and activities, and extract relevant information. These capabilities are crucial for processing and understanding large volumes of visual data from various sources, such as surveillance cameras, social media, and online videos.

Core Concepts

- **Object Detection**: Identifying and locating objects within an image or video frame. Object detection algorithms determine the presence and position of specific objects, such as vehicles, people, or animals.
- **Image Classification**: Categorizing images into predefined classes based on their content. Image classification helps in organizing and managing visual data by assigning labels or categories.
- **Action Recognition**: Identifying and classifying actions or activities in video sequences. Action recognition is used to analyze and interpret dynamic events, such as movements or behaviors.

AI Techniques for Image Recognition

Convolutional Neural Networks (CNNs)

Convolutional Neural Networks (CNNs) are a class of deep learning algorithms specifically designed for processing visual data. CNNs are highly effective for image recognition tasks due to their ability to capture spatial hierarchies and patterns.

- **Architecture**: CNNs consist of multiple layers, including convolutional layers, pooling layers, and fully connected layers. Convolutional layers apply filters to detect features, while pooling layers reduce dimensionality and retain important information.
- **Applications**: CNNs are used for various image recognition tasks, such as object detection, image classification, and facial recognition. They excel at extracting features and identifying patterns in images.

Transfer Learning

Transfer learning involves using pre-trained models on new tasks or datasets. Pre-trained models, such as those trained on large-scale image datasets (e.g., ImageNet), can be fine-tuned for specific image recognition tasks.

- **Fine-Tuning**: Adjusting pre-trained models to adapt to new data or tasks by training on a smaller dataset. Fine-tuning helps leverage existing knowledge and improve performance on specialized tasks.
- **Feature Extraction**: Using pre-trained models as feature extractors to obtain high-level representations of images. These features can be used for classification, detection, or other tasks.

AI Techniques for Video Recognition

Recurrent Neural Networks (RNNs)

Recurrent Neural Networks (RNNs) are designed for sequential data, such as video frames. RNNs can capture temporal dependencies and patterns in video sequences, making them suitable for video recognition tasks.

- **Architecture**: RNNs have feedback connections that allow them to maintain a state across sequences. Long Short-Term Memory (LSTM) networks, a type of RNN, address issues with long-term dependencies and improve performance in video analysis.
- **Applications**: RNNs are used for tasks such as action recognition, event detection, and video summarization. They analyze temporal patterns and sequences to understand dynamic content.

3D Convolutional Networks

3D Convolutional Networks extend traditional 2D CNNs to handle spatiotemporal data by applying convolutions across both spatial and temporal dimensions. This approach captures motion and changes in video sequences.

- **Architecture**: 3D CNNs use 3D convolutions to process video data, combining information from multiple frames. They are effective for detecting actions and events over time.
- **Applications**: 3D CNNs are used for action recognition, event detection, and video classification. They provide a comprehensive analysis of temporal changes in video content.

Applications in OSINT

Surveillance and Security

AI-powered image and video recognition systems enhance surveillance and security operations by analyzing visual data from cameras and sensors.

- **Intrusion Detection**: Identifying unauthorized access or suspicious activities based on visual data from security cameras. AI algorithms detect unusual behaviors or movements and trigger alerts.
- **Facial Recognition**: Identifying and verifying individuals based on facial features. Facial recognition is used for security access control and tracking individuals in surveillance footage.

Social Media and Online Content Analysis

AI techniques analyze images and videos from social media platforms and online sources to gather intelligence and monitor public sentiment.

- **Content Moderation**: Automatically detecting and filtering inappropriate or harmful content in images and videos. AI systems help maintain platform safety and compliance with content policies.
- **Trend Analysis**: Identifying popular trends, themes, and visual content in social media and online platforms. AI algorithms analyze visual data to understand emerging trends and public interests.

Emergency Response and Crisis Management

AI-powered recognition systems support emergency response and crisis management by analyzing visual data from disaster areas or emergency situations.

- **Damage Assessment**: Analyzing satellite or drone images to assess damage caused by natural disasters or accidents. AI systems provide rapid and accurate assessments to support response efforts.
- **Search and Rescue**: Using video data to locate missing persons or survivors in disaster areas. AI algorithms analyze footage from drones or cameras to identify and track individuals.

Challenges and Considerations

Accuracy and Robustness

Ensuring the accuracy and robustness of AI systems in diverse and dynamic environments is a critical challenge. Variability in lighting, angles, and image quality can impact performance.

- **Data Quality**: High-quality training data is essential for accurate recognition. Inadequate or biased data can lead to errors and reduced performance.
- **Generalization**: AI models must generalize well to handle variations in visual data. Techniques such as data augmentation and transfer learning help improve model robustness.

Privacy and Ethical Concerns

The use of AI in image and video recognition raises privacy and ethical concerns, particularly regarding surveillance and data usage.

- **Privacy**: Ensuring that AI systems comply with privacy regulations and protect individuals' personal information. Privacy-preserving techniques and policies are essential for ethical implementation.
- **Bias and Fairness**: Addressing biases in AI models to ensure fair and unbiased recognition. Efforts to identify and mitigate bias are crucial for ethical AI applications.

Computational Resources

AI-powered image and video recognition require significant computational resources, especially for training complex models and processing large volumes of data.

- **Resource Management**: Efficiently managing computational resources and leveraging cloud-based solutions can help address resource demands.
- **Scalability**: Ensuring that AI systems can scale to handle growing data volumes and increasing complexity. Scalable solutions support continuous and effective analysis.

AI has transformed image and video recognition, providing powerful tools for analyzing visual data in Open Source Intelligence (OSINT). By leveraging techniques such as Convolutional Neural Networks (CNNs), Recurrent Neural Networks (RNNs), and 3D Convolutional Networks, AI enhances capabilities in surveillance, social media analysis, and emergency response. While AI offers significant advantages, challenges related to accuracy, privacy, and computational resources must be addressed to ensure effective and ethical implementation. Understanding and applying AI techniques in image and video recognition is essential for harnessing the full potential of visual data analysis in the digital age.

3.4. Automated Pattern Recognition in OSINT

Automated pattern recognition is a cornerstone of modern Open Source Intelligence (OSINT), enabling the extraction of meaningful patterns and trends from vast amounts of unstructured data. By employing advanced algorithms and machine learning techniques, automated pattern recognition transforms raw data into actionable intelligence, facilitating more effective decision-making and insight generation. This section explores the principles, techniques, applications, and challenges of automated pattern recognition in OSINT.

Introduction to Automated Pattern Recognition

Automated pattern recognition involves the use of algorithms and machine learning models to identify recurring patterns, trends, and anomalies within data. This process automates the analysis of complex datasets, providing insights that would be difficult or impossible to discern manually.

Core Concepts

- **Pattern Recognition**: The process of identifying and classifying patterns or regularities in data. In OSINT, pattern recognition helps in detecting trends, anomalies, and relationships within large datasets.
- **Feature Extraction**: The process of transforming raw data into a set of features that can be used for pattern recognition. Feature extraction involves selecting relevant characteristics of the data that are useful for analysis.
- **Classification and Clustering**: Classification involves assigning data points to predefined categories based on their features, while clustering groups similar data points without predefined labels. Both techniques are used for pattern recognition.

Techniques for Automated Pattern Recognition

Machine Learning Approaches

Machine learning algorithms play a crucial role in pattern recognition by learning from data and making predictions or classifications based on identified patterns.

Supervised Learning:

- **Decision Trees**: Tree-like models that split data based on feature values to classify or predict outcomes. Decision trees are used to identify patterns and make decisions based on historical data.
- **Support Vector Machines (SVM):** Algorithms that find the optimal hyperplane to separate different classes. SVMs are effective for detecting patterns in high-dimensional data and classifying them accordingly.
- **Neural Networks**: Models inspired by the human brain, capable of learning complex patterns and relationships in data. Neural networks, including deep learning models, are used for tasks such as image and text classification.

Unsupervised Learning:

- **K-Means Clustering**: An algorithm that partitions data into k clusters based on similarity. K-Means clustering is used to identify groups and patterns within unlabelled data.
- **Hierarchical Clustering**: Builds a hierarchy of clusters by either merging smaller clusters or dividing larger ones. Hierarchical clustering helps in discovering nested patterns and relationships in data.
- **Principal Component Analysis (PCA):** A dimensionality reduction technique that identifies the most important features in the data. PCA helps in revealing patterns by simplifying data while retaining key information.

Anomaly Detection

Anomaly detection focuses on identifying unusual or unexpected patterns that deviate from the norm. This technique is crucial for detecting outliers, fraud, or security threats.

- **Statistical Methods**: Techniques that use statistical models to identify data points that fall outside the expected range. Statistical methods are used to detect anomalies based on distribution and variance.
- **Isolation Forests**: A machine learning algorithm that isolates anomalies by randomly selecting features and splitting data. Isolation forests are effective for detecting anomalies in high-dimensional data.

Deep Learning Approaches

Deep learning models, such as convolutional neural networks (CNNs) and recurrent neural networks (RNNs), offer advanced capabilities for pattern recognition.

- **Convolutional Neural Networks (CNNs):** Used for image and video pattern recognition by learning spatial hierarchies of features. CNNs are effective for identifying patterns in visual data, such as objects and scenes.
- **Recurrent Neural Networks (RNNs):** Designed for sequential data, such as time series or text. RNNs capture temporal patterns and dependencies, making them suitable for recognizing patterns over time.

Applications in OSINT

Threat Detection and Cybersecurity

Automated pattern recognition enhances cybersecurity by detecting and analyzing patterns indicative of potential threats or malicious activities.

- **Intrusion Detection**: Identifying unusual patterns in network traffic that may indicate cyberattacks or unauthorized access. Automated systems analyze traffic patterns to detect anomalies and potential threats.
- **Fraud Detection**: Recognizing patterns of fraudulent behavior in financial transactions or user activities. Automated systems identify deviations from normal patterns to flag potential fraud.

Social Media and Content Analysis

Automated pattern recognition is used to analyze social media and online content for trends, sentiment, and emerging issues.

- **Trend Analysis**: Detecting and analyzing trends in social media posts, hashtags, or online discussions. Automated systems identify patterns in user behavior and content to understand emerging trends.
- **Sentiment Analysis**: Analyzing patterns in user sentiment and opinions expressed in social media or reviews. Automated sentiment analysis provides insights into public perception and reactions.

Market and Competitive Intelligence

Automated pattern recognition helps in analyzing market trends and competitive landscapes by identifying patterns and relationships in business data.

- **Market Trends**: Detecting patterns in sales data, market reports, and consumer behavior. Automated systems identify trends and shifts in market dynamics to support strategic decision-making.
- **Competitor Analysis**: Analyzing patterns in competitor activities, such as product launches or pricing strategies. Automated systems provide insights into competitive positioning and market opportunities.

Emergency Response and Crisis Management

Automated pattern recognition supports emergency response and crisis management by analyzing patterns in data from disaster areas or emergency situations.

- **Damage Assessment**: Identifying patterns in satellite or drone imagery to assess damage from natural disasters or accidents. Automated systems provide rapid assessments to support response efforts.
- **Resource Allocation**: Analyzing patterns in resource usage and distribution during emergencies. Automated systems optimize resource allocation based on identified needs and patterns.

Challenges and Considerations

Data Quality and Quantity

The effectiveness of automated pattern recognition depends on the quality and quantity of data used for training and analysis.

- **Data Quality**: Ensuring that data is accurate, complete, and representative of the patterns being studied. Poor-quality data can lead to inaccurate or misleading results.
- **Data Volume**: Handling large volumes of data requires efficient algorithms and computational resources. Scalability and resource management are crucial for effective pattern recognition.

Complexity and Interpretability

Automated pattern recognition can produce complex models and patterns that may be difficult to interpret or understand.

- **Model Complexity**: Advanced algorithms, such as deep learning models, can be complex and require careful tuning. Ensuring that models are interpretable and understandable is important for practical use.
- **Pattern Interpretation**: Translating identified patterns into actionable insights requires domain expertise and contextual understanding. Effective interpretation of patterns is essential for making informed decisions.

Bias and Fairness

Automated pattern recognition systems can inherit biases present in the training data, affecting their accuracy and fairness.

- **Bias Detection**: Identifying and addressing biases in data and algorithms to ensure fair and unbiased pattern recognition. Efforts to mitigate bias are crucial for ethical and accurate analysis.
- **Fairness**: Ensuring that pattern recognition systems provide equitable and unbiased results across different groups or contexts. Fairness considerations are important for ethical and responsible use.

Automated pattern recognition is a powerful tool in Open Source Intelligence (OSINT), enabling the extraction of meaningful insights from complex and large-scale data. By leveraging machine learning, deep learning, and statistical techniques, automated systems identify patterns, trends, and anomalies that support decision-making and intelligence gathering. While automated pattern recognition offers significant advantages, challenges related to data quality, complexity, and bias must be addressed to ensure effective and ethical analysis. Understanding and applying automated pattern recognition techniques is essential for harnessing the full potential of data-driven intelligence in the digital age.

3.5. Anomaly Detection and Predictive Analytics

Anomaly detection and predictive analytics are powerful tools within Open Source Intelligence (OSINT) that enhance the ability to identify unusual patterns and forecast future trends. These techniques play a critical role in uncovering hidden threats, predicting emerging issues, and making informed decisions based on data-driven insights. This section explores the principles, methods, applications, and challenges of anomaly detection and predictive analytics in OSINT.

Introduction to Anomaly Detection

Anomaly detection involves identifying patterns in data that deviate significantly from the norm. These deviations, or anomalies, can indicate unusual or potentially malicious activities, errors, or outliers in the data. Anomaly detection is crucial for detecting issues that may not be apparent through conventional analysis methods.

Core Concepts

- **Anomaly**: An observation or data point that differs significantly from the expected pattern. Anomalies can be indicative of unusual events, errors, or emerging threats.
- **Baseline**: A reference model or standard used to define what constitutes normal behavior. Baselines are established through historical data and are used to detect deviations.
- **Detection Methods**: Techniques used to identify anomalies, including statistical methods, machine learning algorithms, and hybrid approaches.

Types of Anomalies

- **Point Anomalies**: Individual data points that deviate significantly from the rest of the data. Examples include fraudulent transactions or system errors.
- **Contextual Anomalies**: Data points that are unusual in a specific context or under certain conditions. For example, an increase in network traffic during off-hours may be a contextual anomaly.
- **Collective Anomalies**: Groups or sequences of data points that deviate from the norm. Collective anomalies can indicate patterns of malicious behavior or systemic issues.

Techniques for Anomaly Detection

Statistical Methods

Statistical methods use mathematical models to detect anomalies based on statistical properties of the data. These methods are useful for identifying deviations from expected distributions.

- **Z-Score**: Measures how many standard deviations a data point is from the mean. Z-scores help identify outliers based on their deviation from the mean.

- **Grubbs' Test**: A statistical test used to identify outliers in univariate data. Grubbs' test evaluates whether the most extreme data point is significantly different from the rest.
- **Box Plot Analysis**: A graphical method that uses quartiles to detect outliers. Data points that fall outside the interquartile range are considered anomalies.

Machine Learning Approaches

Machine learning algorithms learn from data to identify patterns and detect anomalies. These approaches are effective for handling complex and high-dimensional data.

- **Isolation Forests**: An ensemble method that isolates anomalies by randomly selecting features and splitting data. Isolation forests are efficient and effective for detecting outliers in high-dimensional datasets.
- **One-Class SVM**: A variation of Support Vector Machines (SVM) designed for anomaly detection. One-Class SVM learns the boundary of normal data and identifies deviations as anomalies.
- **Autoencoders**: Neural networks used for unsupervised anomaly detection. Autoencoders learn to reconstruct input data, and anomalies are detected based on reconstruction errors.

Hybrid Approaches

Hybrid approaches combine multiple techniques to improve the accuracy and robustness of anomaly detection.

- **Statistical and Machine Learning Combination**: Integrating statistical methods with machine learning models to leverage the strengths of both approaches. For example, combining Z-score with Isolation Forests for enhanced detection.
- **Ensemble Methods**: Using multiple anomaly detection algorithms and combining their results to improve overall performance. Ensemble methods help in addressing the limitations of individual techniques.

Introduction to Predictive Analytics

Predictive analytics involves using historical data and statistical algorithms to forecast future trends and outcomes. Predictive models analyze patterns and relationships in data to make predictions about future events or behaviors.

Core Concepts

- **Predictive Modeling**: The process of creating models that use historical data to make forecasts. Predictive models estimate future outcomes based on identified patterns and trends.
- **Features and Variables**: The attributes or factors used in predictive models to make predictions. Features can include historical data, demographic information, or environmental factors.
- **Model Evaluation**: Assessing the performance of predictive models using metrics such as accuracy, precision, recall, and F1-score. Model evaluation helps determine the effectiveness of predictions.

Types of Predictive Models

- **Regression Models**: Predict continuous outcomes based on input features. Common regression techniques include linear regression, polynomial regression, and ridge regression.
- **Classification Models**: Predict categorical outcomes based on input features. Classification techniques include logistic regression, decision trees, and random forests.
- **Time Series Forecasting**: Predict future values based on historical time series data. Time series models, such as ARIMA (AutoRegressive Integrated Moving Average) and exponential smoothing, are used for forecasting.

Applications in OSINT

Threat Detection and Security

Predictive analytics and anomaly detection enhance security by identifying potential threats and vulnerabilities before they escalate.

- **Cybersecurity Threats**: Detecting unusual patterns or anomalies in network traffic, user behavior, or system logs. Predictive models forecast potential security breaches or attacks.
- **Fraud Prevention**: Identifying and predicting fraudulent activities based on historical data and transaction patterns. Anomaly detection helps flag suspicious transactions or behaviors.

Social Media and Sentiment Analysis

Predictive analytics and anomaly detection are used to analyze social media and online content for trends, sentiment, and emerging issues.

- **Trend Prediction**: Forecasting emerging trends and topics based on social media data and user interactions. Predictive models help anticipate shifts in public opinion or interest.
- **Crisis Management**: Identifying and predicting potential crises or issues based on anomaly detection in social media or news data. Predictive analytics supports proactive crisis response.

Market and Competitive Intelligence

Automated pattern recognition supports market analysis and competitive intelligence by forecasting trends and identifying opportunities.

- **Market Trends**: Predicting changes in market conditions, consumer behavior, or sales performance. Predictive models help businesses anticipate market shifts and adjust strategies.
- **Competitor Analysis**: Identifying patterns in competitor activities and forecasting future moves. Predictive analytics provides insights into competitive dynamics and market positioning.

Emergency Response and Resource Management

Predictive analytics and anomaly detection support emergency response and resource management by forecasting needs and assessing impacts.

- **Resource Allocation**: Predicting resource requirements based on historical data and current trends. Predictive models help optimize the allocation of resources during emergencies.
- **Damage Assessment**: Forecasting potential impacts of disasters based on historical data and real-time observations. Predictive analytics supports rapid and effective response efforts.

Challenges and Considerations

Data Quality and Availability

The effectiveness of anomaly detection and predictive analytics relies on the quality and availability of data.

- **Data Quality**: Ensuring that data is accurate, complete, and representative of the patterns being analyzed. Poor-quality data can lead to inaccurate predictions and detections.
- **Data Availability**: Accessing sufficient data for training and validation of models. Limited or incomplete data can affect the performance of predictive models and anomaly detection.

Model Complexity and Interpretability

Advanced models may be complex and difficult to interpret, posing challenges for understanding and explaining results.

- **Model Complexity**: Balancing model complexity with interpretability. Complex models, such as deep learning, may offer high accuracy but can be challenging to understand and explain.
- **Interpretability**: Ensuring that predictions and detections are understandable and actionable. Transparent and interpretable models help in making informed decisions based on insights.

Bias and Fairness

Addressing biases in data and models is crucial for ensuring fair and accurate results.

- **Bias Detection**: Identifying and mitigating biases present in training data or models. Bias can lead to unfair or discriminatory outcomes in predictions and detections.
- **Fairness**: Ensuring that models provide equitable results across different groups or contexts. Fairness considerations are important for ethical and responsible use of predictive analytics and anomaly detection.

Computational Resources

Implementing anomaly detection and predictive analytics requires significant computational resources, particularly for large-scale data.

- **Resource Management**: Efficiently managing computational resources and leveraging cloud-based solutions. Scalable solutions support continuous and effective analysis.

- **Scalability**: Ensuring that models and systems can handle growing data volumes and increasing complexity. Scalable solutions are essential for maintaining performance and accuracy.

Anomaly detection and predictive analytics are essential components of Open Source Intelligence (OSINT), providing powerful tools for identifying unusual patterns and forecasting future trends. By leveraging statistical methods, machine learning, and deep learning approaches, these techniques enhance the ability to detect threats, predict emerging issues, and make data-driven decisions. While anomaly detection and predictive analytics offer significant advantages, challenges related to data quality, model complexity, and bias must be addressed to ensure effective and ethical analysis. Understanding and applying these techniques is crucial for harnessing the full potential of data-driven intelligence in the modern era.

Chapter 4: OSINT Tools Powered by AI

Chapter 4, "OSINT Tools Powered by AI," provides an in-depth look at the advanced tools and platforms that are driving the next generation of Open Source Intelligence (OSINT). This chapter explores a range of AI-powered tools, detailing their key features, capabilities, and practical applications in cyber investigations. Through comparative analysis and real-world examples, readers will gain insight into how these tools leverage AI to automate data collection, enhance analysis, and deliver more accurate and timely intelligence. As AI continues to reshape the OSINT landscape, understanding these tools is crucial for professionals seeking to harness their full potential in the fight against cyber threats.

4.1. Overview of AI-Driven OSINT Tools

AI-driven Open Source Intelligence (OSINT) tools represent a significant advancement in the field of intelligence gathering and analysis. By leveraging artificial intelligence (AI) technologies, these tools enhance the ability to collect, analyze, and interpret large volumes of data from diverse sources. This section provides an overview of AI-driven OSINT tools, highlighting their capabilities, benefits, and examples.

Introduction to AI-Driven OSINT Tools

AI-driven OSINT tools integrate artificial intelligence techniques with traditional OSINT methods to improve data collection, analysis, and decision-making processes. These tools use AI to automate and augment various aspects of intelligence gathering, enabling more efficient and accurate insights.

Core Components of AI-Driven OSINT Tools

- **Data Collection**: The process of gathering data from various open sources, such as websites, social media, forums, and public records. AI-driven tools can automate data collection and aggregate information from multiple sources.
- **Data Processing**: The transformation of raw data into structured formats suitable for analysis. AI techniques, such as Natural Language Processing (NLP) and image recognition, are used to process and extract relevant information.
- **Data Analysis**: The examination of processed data to identify patterns, trends, and anomalies. AI algorithms, including machine learning and predictive

analytics, enhance the analysis by providing deeper insights and automated decision-making.

- **Reporting and Visualization**: The presentation of analyzed data in formats that are easy to understand and interpret. AI-driven tools often include features for generating reports, dashboards, and visualizations to support decision-making.

Capabilities of AI-Driven OSINT Tools

Enhanced Data Collection

AI-driven OSINT tools automate and streamline the process of collecting data from various sources, increasing efficiency and coverage.

- **Web Scraping**: Automated extraction of data from websites and online platforms. AI-driven scraping tools can navigate complex web structures and extract relevant information, such as text, images, and metadata.
- **Social Media Monitoring**: Tracking and analyzing social media activity to gather real-time insights. AI tools monitor social media platforms for specific keywords, hashtags, or user activities, providing timely information on trends and sentiments.
- **Sentiment Analysis**: Using AI to analyze the sentiment expressed in text data. Sentiment analysis tools assess the emotional tone of social media posts, reviews, and news articles, helping to gauge public opinion and reactions.

Advanced Data Processing

AI technologies enhance the processing of raw data, enabling the extraction of meaningful information from unstructured sources.

- **Natural Language Processing (NLP):** Analyzing and understanding human language in text data. NLP techniques are used for tasks such as entity recognition, language translation, and text summarization.
- **Image and Video Analysis**: Using AI algorithms to analyze visual content. Tools equipped with image recognition and video analysis capabilities can identify objects, faces, and activities within images and videos.
- **Data Enrichment**: Enhancing collected data with additional context and information. AI-driven tools can integrate external datasets and perform cross-referencing to provide a more comprehensive view.

Sophisticated Data Analysis

AI-driven analysis tools provide deeper insights by identifying patterns, trends, and anomalies in large datasets.

- **Machine Learning Algorithms**: Applying machine learning models to identify patterns and make predictions. Algorithms such as clustering, classification, and regression are used to analyze data and uncover insights.
- **Anomaly Detection**: Detecting deviations from normal patterns to identify unusual or suspicious activities. AI-powered anomaly detection tools can flag potential threats or irregularities based on historical data.
- **Predictive Analytics:** Forecasting future trends and outcomes based on historical data. Predictive models use AI to estimate future events, such as emerging threats or market shifts.

Comprehensive Reporting and Visualization

AI-driven OSINT tools offer advanced reporting and visualization features to present analyzed data in a clear and actionable manner.

- **Dashboards**: Interactive interfaces that display key metrics, trends, and insights. Dashboards provide real-time updates and allow users to explore data through various visualizations.
- **Data Visualizations**: Graphs, charts, and maps that represent data visually. AI tools generate visualizations to help users understand complex data and identify patterns more easily.
- **Automated Reporting**: Generating reports based on analyzed data. AI-driven tools can create detailed reports with summaries, findings, and recommendations, reducing the need for manual report generation.

Examples of AI-Driven OSINT Tools

Data Collection Tools

- **Scrapy**: An open-source web scraping framework that uses AI to extract data from websites. Scrapy can be customized to collect information from various sources and handle dynamic content.
- **Hootsuite Insights**: A social media monitoring tool that uses AI to analyze social media activity. Hootsuite Insights tracks keywords, hashtags, and sentiment to provide insights into social media trends.

Data Processing Tools

- **Google Cloud Vision**: An AI-powered image recognition tool that analyzes images and extracts information. Google Cloud Vision can identify objects, text, and faces within images.
- **IBM Watson NLP**: A Natural Language Processing tool that analyzes and interprets text data. IBM Watson NLP performs tasks such as sentiment analysis, entity recognition, and language translation.

Data Analysis Tools

- **RapidMiner**: A data science platform that uses machine learning algorithms for data analysis. RapidMiner supports various analytics tasks, including clustering, classification, and predictive modeling.
- **Splunk**: A platform for searching, monitoring, and analyzing machine-generated data. Splunk uses AI to detect anomalies, perform predictive analytics, and generate insights from log data.

Reporting and Visualization Tools

- **Tableau**: A data visualization tool that creates interactive dashboards and reports. Tableau integrates with AI-driven analysis tools to provide visual representations of data insights.
- **Power BI**: A business analytics tool that offers reporting and visualization features. Power BI uses AI to enhance data analysis and create comprehensive visualizations.

Benefits of AI-Driven OSINT Tools

Increased Efficiency

AI-driven tools automate time-consuming tasks, such as data collection and processing, allowing analysts to focus on more strategic activities.

Improved Accuracy

AI algorithms reduce human error and provide more accurate insights by analyzing large volumes of data with precision.

Enhanced Insight Generation

AI-driven tools identify patterns, trends, and anomalies that may be overlooked by traditional methods, providing deeper and more actionable insights.

Real-Time Analysis

AI tools enable real-time monitoring and analysis, allowing for timely responses to emerging threats or opportunities.

Challenges and Considerations

Data Privacy and Security

Handling sensitive or personal data requires adherence to privacy regulations and ensuring that data is protected from unauthorized access.

Bias and Fairness

AI algorithms can inherit biases from training data, leading to unfair or inaccurate results. Ensuring fairness and mitigating bias is essential for reliable analysis.

Complexity and Integration

Integrating AI-driven tools with existing systems and workflows can be complex. Ensuring compatibility and effective integration is crucial for maximizing the benefits of these tools.

Cost and Resource Requirements

Implementing and maintaining AI-driven OSINT tools may involve significant costs and resource allocation. Evaluating the return on investment and resource requirements is important for decision-making.

AI-driven OSINT tools represent a significant advancement in the field of intelligence gathering and analysis. By leveraging artificial intelligence technologies, these tools enhance the efficiency, accuracy, and depth of data collection, processing, and analysis. Understanding the capabilities, benefits, and challenges of AI-driven OSINT tools is crucial for effectively harnessing their potential and making informed decisions based on data-driven insights.

4.2. Key Features of AI-Enhanced OSINT Platforms

AI-enhanced OSINT (Open Source Intelligence) platforms leverage artificial intelligence to transform how intelligence is collected, processed, and analyzed. These platforms offer a range of advanced features designed to improve the efficiency, accuracy, and depth of intelligence operations. This section explores the key features of AI-enhanced OSINT platforms, highlighting how they contribute to more effective intelligence gathering and analysis.

1. Automated Data Collection

AI-enhanced OSINT platforms streamline and automate the process of collecting data from diverse sources, reducing the need for manual intervention and increasing the scope of data collection.

Web Scraping and Crawling

- **Automated Extraction**: AI-driven tools can automatically extract data from websites, online forums, social media platforms, and other web-based sources.
- **Dynamic Content Handling**: AI platforms can handle dynamic and JavaScript-generated content, ensuring comprehensive data collection from modern web applications.

Social Media Monitoring

- **Real-Time Tracking**: AI tools monitor social media platforms in real-time, capturing posts, comments, hashtags, and mentions.
- **Sentiment Analysis**: AI algorithms analyze the sentiment expressed in social media content, providing insights into public opinion and trends.

Multilingual Support

- **Language Detection**: AI platforms can detect and process multiple languages, enabling the collection of data from international sources.
- **Translation Capabilities**: Integrated translation features allow for the conversion of foreign language content into the user's preferred language.

2. Advanced Data Processing

AI-enhanced OSINT platforms utilize sophisticated data processing techniques to transform raw data into structured, actionable information.

Natural Language Processing (NLP)

- **Entity Recognition**: AI identifies and extracts entities such as people, organizations, locations, and events from text data.
- **Text Summarization**: NLP algorithms generate concise summaries of lengthy documents or articles, highlighting key points and relevant information.

Image and Video Analysis

- **Object Detection**: AI-driven image recognition identifies and categorizes objects, people, and scenes within visual content.
- **Facial Recognition**: Advanced facial recognition technology can identify individuals in images and videos, supporting investigations and tracking.

Data Enrichment

- **Contextualization**: AI platforms enrich collected data with additional context from related sources, enhancing the depth of analysis.
- **Cross-Referencing**: Integration with external databases and datasets allows for cross-referencing and validation of collected information.

3. Intelligent Data Analysis

AI-enhanced OSINT platforms offer advanced analytical capabilities to uncover patterns, trends, and insights from large volumes of data.

Machine Learning Algorithms

- **Pattern Recognition**: Machine learning models identify patterns and correlations within data, providing insights into trends and anomalies.
- **Clustering and Classification**: AI algorithms group similar data points and classify them into predefined categories, aiding in the organization and interpretation of data.

Anomaly Detection

- **Real-Time Alerts**: AI-driven anomaly detection systems identify deviations from normal patterns and generate real-time alerts for unusual or suspicious activities.
- **Historical Comparison**: Anomaly detection tools compare current data with historical trends to identify emerging threats or significant changes.

Predictive Analytics

- **Trend Forecasting**: Predictive models estimate future trends and outcomes based on historical data and current observations.
- **Risk Assessment**: AI platforms assess potential risks and threats by analyzing data patterns and predicting future scenarios.

4. Comprehensive Reporting and Visualization

AI-enhanced OSINT platforms provide sophisticated reporting and visualization tools to present analyzed data in a clear, actionable format.

Customizable Dashboards

- **Interactive Interfaces**: Dashboards offer interactive and customizable interfaces for users to view key metrics, trends, and insights.
- **Real-Time Data Display**: Dashboards update in real-time, providing current information and facilitating dynamic analysis.

Data Visualization

- **Charts and Graphs**: AI platforms generate various types of charts and graphs to represent data visually, aiding in the interpretation of complex information.
- **Geospatial Mapping**: Visualization tools include geospatial mapping features to display location-based data and spatial relationships.

Automated Reporting

- **Report Generation**: AI-driven platforms can automatically generate detailed reports based on analyzed data, including summaries, findings, and recommendations.
- **Scheduled Reports**: Users can schedule regular reports to be generated and distributed at specified intervals, ensuring timely updates.

5. Integration and Scalability

AI-enhanced OSINT platforms are designed to integrate with existing systems and scale to handle large volumes of data.

API Integration

- **System Integration**: Platforms offer APIs for seamless integration with other tools and systems, enabling data sharing and interoperability.
- **Custom Connectors**: Custom connectors allow for the integration of specific data sources or platforms according to user needs.

Scalability

- **Handling Large Data Volumes**: AI platforms are designed to handle and process large volumes of data efficiently, supporting scalability for growing intelligence requirements.
- **Cloud-Based Solutions**: Many AI-enhanced OSINT tools utilize cloud-based infrastructure, providing flexibility and scalability for data storage and processing.

6. Security and Compliance

AI-enhanced OSINT platforms prioritize security and compliance to protect data and adhere to regulatory standards.

Data Encryption

- **Encryption Standards**: AI platforms use encryption to secure data during transmission and storage, protecting it from unauthorized access.
- **Access Controls**: Role-based access controls ensure that only authorized users can access sensitive data and features.

Compliance with Regulations

- **Data Privacy**: Platforms comply with data privacy regulations, such as GDPR and CCPA, ensuring the protection of personal information.
- **Audit Trails**: AI systems maintain audit trails to track access and changes to data, supporting accountability and transparency.

AI-enhanced OSINT platforms offer a range of advanced features that transform the process of intelligence gathering and analysis. By automating data collection, utilizing sophisticated processing techniques, and providing intelligent analysis, these platforms enable more efficient and accurate intelligence operations. Key features such as automated data collection, advanced processing, intelligent analysis, comprehensive reporting, integration, scalability, and security contribute to the effectiveness of AI-driven OSINT tools. Understanding these features is essential for leveraging the full potential of AI in modern intelligence practices.

4.3. Comparative Analysis of Popular AI-OSINT Tools

In the rapidly evolving field of Open Source Intelligence (OSINT), AI-driven tools have become indispensable for gathering, processing, and analyzing vast amounts of data. With a multitude of AI-OSINT tools available, selecting the right one depends on various factors, including features, capabilities, ease of use, and cost. This comparative analysis examines several popular AI-OSINT tools, highlighting their strengths, weaknesses, and ideal use cases.

1. Palantir Foundry

Overview: Palantir Foundry is a comprehensive data integration and analysis platform that utilizes AI to provide deep insights and support complex investigations.

Strengths:

- **Data Integration**: Palantir excels in integrating data from diverse sources, including structured and unstructured data.
- **Advanced Analytics**: Offers sophisticated analytics capabilities, including machine learning models and predictive analytics.
- **Customizability**: Highly customizable with extensive features for data visualization, reporting, and workflow management.

Weaknesses:

- **Complexity**: The platform's extensive features and customization options can lead to a steep learning curve.
- **Cost**: Palantir Foundry is often considered expensive, which may be a barrier for smaller organizations.
- **Ideal Use Case**: Suitable for large organizations and government agencies requiring robust data integration and complex analytics for investigative and strategic purposes.

2. IBM i2 Analyst's Notebook

Overview: IBM i2 Analyst's Notebook is a visual analysis tool that uses AI to enhance investigative capabilities through data visualization and pattern recognition.

Strengths:

- **Visualization**: Known for its powerful data visualization and link analysis features, making it easier to uncover relationships and patterns.
- **Intuitive Interface**: Provides a user-friendly interface that simplifies complex data analysis tasks.
- **Integration**: Integrates well with other data sources and analytics tools.

Weaknesses:

- **Learning Curve**: While user-friendly, mastering advanced features and capabilities may require additional training.
- **Cost**: Pricing can be high, potentially limiting accessibility for smaller organizations.
- **Ideal Use Case**: Best suited for law enforcement, intelligence agencies, and analysts who need advanced visualization and link analysis capabilities for complex investigations.

3. Recorded Future

Overview: Recorded Future specializes in threat intelligence, using AI to collect and analyze data from open sources, including the dark web, to provide actionable insights on emerging threats.

Strengths:

- **Threat Intelligence**: Excellent at identifying and analyzing threats from a wide range of sources, including dark web forums and social media.
- **Real-Time Data**: Provides real-time threat intelligence and alerts based on current data and trends.
- **Ease of Use**: User-friendly interface with actionable insights and customizable alerts.

Weaknesses:

- **Focus**: Primarily focused on threat intelligence, which may limit its utility for broader OSINT tasks.
- **Data Overload**: The volume of data and alerts can be overwhelming, requiring effective filtering and management.
- **Ideal Use Case**: Ideal for cybersecurity teams and threat analysts who need real-time intelligence on potential threats and vulnerabilities.

4. Maltego

Overview: Maltego is a data mining tool that uses AI to visualize relationships and networks between different data points, facilitating link analysis and information gathering.

Strengths:

- **Link Analysis**: Strong capabilities for visualizing relationships and networks, making it valuable for investigative research.
- **Customization**: Offers a range of transforms and extensions for customizing data collection and analysis.
- **Community Integration**: Supports integration with various third-party data sources and platforms.

Weaknesses:

- **Learning Curve**: The extensive range of features and customization options can be challenging for new users to master.
- **Performance**: Performance can be affected by the complexity of the queries and the volume of data being processed.
- **Ideal Use Case**: Suitable for investigators, cybersecurity professionals, and analysts who require in-depth link analysis and network visualization for their OSINT activities.

5. Social-Engineer Toolkit (SET)

Overview: The Social-Engineer Toolkit (SET) is an open-source tool designed for social engineering attacks and penetration testing, with AI enhancements for analyzing and simulating social engineering scenarios.

Strengths:

- **Social Engineering**: Effective for simulating social engineering attacks and assessing vulnerabilities in security awareness.
- **Customization**: Highly customizable with various attack vectors and simulation options.
- **Open Source**: Free to use and continually updated by the community.

Weaknesses:

- **Specialized Focus**: Primarily focused on social engineering and penetration testing, which may limit its use for broader OSINT tasks.
- **Complexity**: Requires a good understanding of social engineering techniques and methodologies.
- **Ideal Use Case**: Best for security professionals and penetration testers who need to simulate social engineering attacks and assess vulnerabilities in security practices.

6. DataMiner

Overview: DataMiner is a web scraping tool that uses AI to extract data from websites and online sources, enabling users to gather information for various analytical purposes.

Strengths:

- **Ease of Use**: User-friendly interface with simple configuration options for web scraping tasks.
- **Versatility**: Supports a wide range of websites and data formats, making it versatile for different data collection needs.
- **Customization**: Offers customizable scraping rules and automation features.

Weaknesses:

- **Scalability**: May face limitations when dealing with very large volumes of data or highly dynamic websites.
- **Data Accuracy**: The accuracy of scraped data can vary depending on website structure and changes.
- **Ideal Use Case**: Suitable for researchers, analysts, and data scientists who need to collect data from websites and online sources for analysis and reporting.

7. Echosec

Overview: Echosec is a geospatial intelligence platform that uses AI to analyze social media and other open sources, providing insights into location-based data and trends.

Strengths:

- **Geospatial Analysis**: Strong capabilities in analyzing location-based data and visualizing geospatial trends.
- **Real-Time Monitoring**: Provides real-time updates and alerts based on geospatial data from social media and other sources.
- **User-Friendly Interface**: Intuitive interface for exploring and analyzing geospatial information.

Weaknesses:

- **Specialization**: Focused primarily on geospatial intelligence, which may limit its application for other types of OSINT tasks.
- **Data Integration**: May face challenges in integrating with some data sources or platforms.
- **Ideal Use Case**: Ideal for organizations and analysts who require geospatial insights and location-based analysis for security, intelligence, and research purposes.

Each AI-enhanced OSINT tool offers unique features and capabilities, making them suitable for different use cases and organizational needs. Palantir Foundry and IBM i2 Analyst's Notebook excel in data integration and visualization, respectively, while Recorded Future and Maltego provide specialized capabilities for threat intelligence and link analysis. Tools like SET and DataMiner focus on social engineering and web scraping, respectively, offering specialized functionalities. Echosec stands out for its geospatial intelligence capabilities. Choosing the right AI-OSINT tool depends on specific requirements, including the nature of the intelligence work, data sources, and analysis needs. Evaluating these factors will help organizations select the most appropriate tool for their OSINT activities.

4.4. Customizing AI Tools for Specific Investigations

Customizing AI tools for specific investigations is crucial for tailoring their functionality to meet particular requirements and challenges. This customization enhances the effectiveness of AI-driven OSINT (Open Source Intelligence) tools by adapting them to the unique aspects of each investigation. This section explores the various strategies and methods for customizing AI tools, including setting parameters, integrating with other systems, developing custom algorithms, and optimizing data handling.

1. Defining Investigation Objectives and Requirements

Before customizing AI tools, it's essential to clearly define the objectives and requirements of the investigation. This involves:

Understanding Investigation Goals

- **Specific Objectives**: Identify the precise goals of the investigation, such as detecting threats, uncovering fraud, or analyzing social media trends.
- **Scope and Focus**: Determine the scope of the investigation, including the types of data and sources that are most relevant.

Data Requirements

- **Types of Data**: Specify the types of data needed, such as text, images, videos, or geospatial information.
- **Data Sources**: Identify the sources from which data will be collected, including websites, social media platforms, and databases.

2. Configuring Tool Parameters

Customizing AI tools often involves configuring parameters to align with the specific needs of the investigation. This includes:

Data Collection Settings

- **Source Filters**: Set filters to target specific data sources or types of content. For example, configure web scraping tools to extract data only from relevant websites or social media platforms.
- **Frequency and Timing**: Adjust settings for data collection frequency and timing to ensure timely and relevant data is gathered.

Processing Parameters

- **Language and Localization**: Configure language settings and localization options to handle data in different languages or regional contexts.

- **Data Extraction Rules**: Define rules for extracting relevant information from unstructured data, such as identifying key entities or sentiment.

Analysis Criteria

- **Algorithm Tuning**: Adjust machine learning algorithms and models to focus on specific patterns or anomalies relevant to the investigation.
- **Thresholds and Sensitivity**: Set thresholds and sensitivity levels for detecting anomalies or generating alerts based on investigation criteria.

3. Integrating with Other Systems

Customizing AI tools may require integration with other systems and platforms to enhance functionality and data accessibility:

Data Integration

- **APIs and Connectors**: Use APIs and connectors to integrate AI tools with existing databases, CRM systems, or other data sources.
- **Data Feeds**: Configure data feeds to ensure seamless integration and real-time data flow between systems.

Collaboration and Reporting

- **Collaboration Tools**: Integrate with collaboration platforms to facilitate team communication and information sharing during the investigation.
- **Reporting Systems**: Connect with reporting tools to generate customized reports and visualizations based on the investigation's findings.

Workflow Automation

- **Automated Processes**: Set up automated workflows to streamline repetitive tasks, such as data collection, analysis, and reporting.
- **Alerts and Notifications**: Configure automated alerts and notifications to inform stakeholders of critical findings or changes in data.

4. Developing Custom Algorithms and Models

For highly specialized investigations, developing custom algorithms and models may be necessary to address specific requirements:

Custom Machine Learning Models

- **Training Data**: Gather and prepare training data specific to the investigation's focus to develop custom machine learning models.
- **Model Development**: Develop and train custom models to detect specific patterns, classify data, or make predictions relevant to the investigation.

Algorithm Adaptation

- **Feature Engineering**: Customize algorithms by selecting and engineering features that are most relevant to the investigation's objectives.
- **Model Optimization**: Fine-tune model parameters and algorithms to improve accuracy and performance for the specific use case.

Integration with Existing Models

- **Hybrid Models**: Integrate custom models with existing AI tools to enhance overall performance and address specialized needs.
- **Model Updating**: Regularly update and retrain models based on new data and evolving investigation requirements.

5. Optimizing Data Handling and Storage

Efficient data handling and storage are critical for the effectiveness of AI-driven investigations:

Data Storage Solutions

- **Scalable Storage**: Choose scalable storage solutions to handle large volumes of data collected during the investigation.
- **Data Management**: Implement data management practices to organize and catalog data for easy retrieval and analysis.

Data Quality and Integrity

- **Data Cleaning**: Perform data cleaning and validation to ensure the accuracy and reliability of the data used in the investigation.
- **Data Security**: Implement security measures to protect sensitive data and maintain confidentiality throughout the investigation.

Performance Optimization

- **Resource Allocation**: Optimize resource allocation to ensure efficient processing and analysis of data.
- **Performance Monitoring**: Monitor the performance of AI tools and make adjustments as needed to address any issues or inefficiencies.

6. Testing and Validation

Customizing AI tools requires thorough testing and validation to ensure they meet the investigation's requirements:

Pilot Testing

- **Test Scenarios**: Run pilot tests using sample data and scenarios to evaluate the effectiveness of the customized tools.
- **Feedback and Adjustment**: Gather feedback from users and make necessary adjustments to improve tool performance and accuracy.

Validation and Evaluation

- **Performance Metrics**: Assess the performance of the customized tools based on metrics such as accuracy, speed, and relevance.
- **Continuous Improvement**: Continuously evaluate and refine the customization to adapt to changing investigation needs and data trends.

Customizing AI tools for specific investigations involves configuring parameters, integrating with other systems, developing custom algorithms, and optimizing data handling. By tailoring AI tools to meet the unique requirements of each investigation, organizations can enhance their intelligence gathering and analysis capabilities. Defining clear objectives, integrating with existing systems, developing specialized models, and conducting thorough testing are essential steps in ensuring that AI tools effectively support the investigation and provide actionable insights.

4.5. Case Studies: AI Tools in Action

Case studies provide practical insights into how AI-driven OSINT (Open Source Intelligence) tools are applied in real-world scenarios. They illustrate the effectiveness of these tools in solving complex problems, enhancing investigations, and supporting decision-making. This section explores several case studies that demonstrate the diverse applications of AI tools in various fields, including cybersecurity, law enforcement, corporate intelligence, and threat analysis.

1. Case Study: Enhancing Cybersecurity with AI-Driven Threat Intelligence

Context: A multinational corporation faced increasing cyber threats from sophisticated threat actors targeting their network infrastructure. The company needed a robust solution to identify and mitigate potential threats in real-time.

AI Tool Used: Recorded Future

Application:

- **Real-Time Threat Intelligence**: Recorded Future was deployed to monitor and analyze data from open sources, including social media, dark web forums, and threat databases.
- **Automated Alerts**: The tool provided real-time alerts on emerging threats and vulnerabilities based on the latest intelligence.
- **Risk Assessment**: AI algorithms assessed the severity and potential impact of identified threats, helping the security team prioritize their response.

Outcome:

- **Increased Detection**: The company improved its ability to detect and respond to threats before they could exploit vulnerabilities.
- **Proactive Defense**: With actionable intelligence and automated alerts, the cybersecurity team could take proactive measures to protect the network.
- **Enhanced Incident Response**: The real-time insights facilitated quicker decision-making and more effective incident response.

2. Case Study: Law Enforcement Investigation Using AI-Powered Link Analysis

Context: A law enforcement agency was investigating a complex organized crime network involving multiple individuals and entities. The goal was to uncover hidden connections and gather evidence for prosecution.

AI Tool Used: IBM i2 Analyst's Notebook

Application:

- **Link Analysis**: The tool was used to visualize and analyze relationships between individuals, organizations, and activities involved in the criminal network.
- **Data Integration**: Data from various sources, including surveillance reports, financial records, and witness statements, was integrated into the platform.
- **Pattern Recognition**: AI algorithms identified patterns and connections that were not immediately apparent to investigators.

Outcome:

- **Uncovered Connections**: The visualization and link analysis revealed previously unknown connections between key figures in the criminal network.
- **Strengthened Case**: The detailed analysis provided crucial evidence that supported the prosecution's case.
- **Efficient Investigation**: The tool streamlined the investigative process, allowing the team to focus on high-priority leads and evidence.

3. Case Study: Corporate Intelligence with AI-Powered Competitive Analysis

Context: A global corporation sought to gain a competitive edge by analyzing the market strategies and activities of its competitors. The goal was to identify emerging trends and potential threats to its market position.

AI Tool Used: Palantir Foundry

Application:

- **Data Integration**: Palantir Foundry was used to integrate and analyze data from various sources, including market reports, financial statements, and news articles.
- **Trend Analysis**: AI algorithms analyzed market trends, competitor activities, and strategic moves to provide actionable insights.
- **Scenario Modeling**: The tool was used to model different scenarios and predict potential impacts on the corporation's market position.

Outcome:

- **Strategic Insights**: The analysis provided valuable insights into competitors' strategies, helping the corporation adjust its own market approach.

- **Informed Decision-Making**: The predictive modeling enabled the corporation to anticipate market changes and make informed strategic decisions.
- **Competitive Advantage**: The corporation gained a competitive advantage by staying ahead of market trends and competitor actions.

4. Case Study: Investigating Financial Fraud with AI-Driven Data Analysis

Context: An auditing firm was tasked with investigating a case of suspected financial fraud involving multiple transactions and accounts. The objective was to identify irregularities and uncover fraudulent activities.

AI Tool Used: DataMiner

Application:

- **Data Extraction**: DataMiner was used to scrape and extract financial data from various online sources, including transaction records and account statements.
- **Pattern Detection**: AI algorithms analyzed transaction patterns to detect anomalies and suspicious activities.
- **Fraud Detection**: The tool identified patterns indicative of fraudulent behavior, such as unusual transaction volumes and atypical account activities.

Outcome:

- **Fraud Identification**: The analysis revealed several instances of fraudulent transactions and irregularities within the financial records.
- **Evidence Collection**: The tool provided detailed evidence that supported the investigation and legal proceedings.
- **Improved Accuracy**: The use of AI-driven analysis improved the accuracy and efficiency of the fraud detection process.

5. Case Study: Geospatial Intelligence for Crisis Management

Context: During a natural disaster, emergency response teams needed real-time information on affected areas to coordinate rescue and relief efforts effectively.

AI Tool Used: Echosec

Application:

- **Geospatial Analysis**: Echosec was used to analyze geospatial data from social media posts, satellite images, and other sources.
- **Real-Time Mapping**: The tool provided real-time maps highlighting areas affected by the disaster and locations of reported incidents.
- **Resource Allocation**: The geospatial insights helped in prioritizing resource deployment and coordinating response efforts.

Outcome:

- **Enhanced Response**: The real-time geospatial analysis enabled more effective and targeted response to the disaster.
- **Improved Coordination**: Emergency teams were able to coordinate their efforts based on accurate and timely information.
- **Efficient Resource Use**: Resources were allocated more efficiently, leading to a more effective disaster response.

6. Case Study: Social Media Analysis for Public Sentiment Research

Context: A research organization wanted to understand public sentiment and opinions on a major political event. The goal was to gather insights from social media platforms to gauge public reaction.

AI Tool Used: Maltego

Application:

- **Social Media Analysis**: Maltego was used to analyze social media content, including posts, comments, and hashtags related to the political event.
- **Sentiment Analysis**: AI algorithms performed sentiment analysis to determine the overall public sentiment and identify key themes.
- **Network Mapping**: The tool mapped networks of social media influencers and key opinion leaders to understand their impact on public sentiment.

Outcome:

- **Insightful Data**: The analysis provided valuable insights into public sentiment, highlighting both positive and negative reactions.
- **Trend Identification**: Key trends and themes related to the political event were identified, aiding in understanding public opinion.

- **Influence Assessment**: The mapping of social media networks helped assess the influence of key figures on public sentiment.

These case studies illustrate the diverse applications and benefits of AI-driven OSINT tools across various domains. From enhancing cybersecurity and supporting law enforcement investigations to providing competitive analysis and geospatial intelligence, AI tools offer valuable capabilities that address complex challenges and improve decision-making. By examining these real-world examples, organizations can gain insights into how AI tools can be effectively utilized to meet specific objectives and enhance their intelligence and analytical capabilities.

Chapter 5: Real-Time Threat Intelligence

Chapter 5, "Real-Time Threat Intelligence," focuses on the dynamic role of Artificial Intelligence (AI) in enabling real-time monitoring and analysis of cyber threats. This chapter explores how AI-driven OSINT tools are used to track and assess emerging threats across various platforms, including social media, forums, and the dark web. By leveraging AI's ability to process large volumes of data instantaneously, these tools provide investigators with timely and actionable intelligence, allowing them to anticipate and respond to threats before they escalate. The chapter emphasizes the importance of real-time intelligence in today's rapidly evolving cyber landscape, where staying ahead of adversaries is more critical than ever.

5.1. Monitoring Social Media with AI

Social media has become a critical source of real-time information and public sentiment, making it an essential component of modern intelligence and threat analysis. AI-powered tools enhance the ability to monitor, analyze, and act upon social media data, providing valuable insights for various applications, including cybersecurity, brand management, and crisis response. This section explores the techniques and benefits of using AI for social media monitoring, highlighting key methodologies and tools that transform raw social media data into actionable intelligence.

1. Importance of Social Media Monitoring

Social media platforms, such as Twitter, Facebook, Instagram, and LinkedIn, generate vast amounts of user-generated content daily. This data is invaluable for several reasons:

Real-Time Insights: Social media provides real-time information about public opinions, trends, and emerging issues. Monitoring these platforms helps organizations stay informed about current events and public sentiment.

Threat Detection: Social media can reveal early warning signs of potential threats, including security breaches, fraudulent activities, or crises. Monitoring these signals allows for timely intervention.

Brand Reputation Management: Organizations can track mentions of their brand or products to manage their reputation and address customer feedback or complaints effectively.

Market Research: Social media data offers insights into consumer preferences and behaviors, aiding in market research and competitive analysis.

2. Techniques for AI-Driven Social Media Monitoring

AI enhances social media monitoring through various techniques, each contributing to the effective extraction and analysis of relevant information:

Natural Language Processing (NLP)

- **Text Analysis**: NLP algorithms analyze text to identify and understand the content of social media posts. Techniques include sentiment analysis, entity recognition, and topic modeling.
- **Sentiment Analysis**: AI models assess the sentiment of social media posts (positive, negative, or neutral) to gauge public opinion on various topics.
- **Emotion Detection**: Advanced NLP techniques can detect specific emotions expressed in social media content, such as anger, joy, or sadness.

Image and Video Recognition

- **Content Analysis**: AI-powered image and video recognition tools analyze visual content shared on social media. This includes identifying objects, people, and logos, as well as detecting potentially harmful content.
- **Contextual Understanding**: AI models understand the context of images and videos to extract meaningful information and identify relevant patterns.

Trend Analysis

- **Hashtag and Keyword Tracking**: AI tools track hashtags and keywords to identify trending topics and conversations across social media platforms.
- **Network Analysis**: Social network analysis tools map relationships between users and detect influential individuals or groups driving specific trends.

Anomaly Detection

- **Behavioral Patterns**: AI algorithms analyze user behavior to detect anomalies, such as sudden spikes in activity or unusual posting patterns, which may indicate potential threats or emerging issues.
- **Fraud Detection**: AI tools identify suspicious behavior, such as fake accounts or coordinated misinformation campaigns, by analyzing posting patterns and engagement metrics.

3. Tools for AI-Driven Social Media Monitoring

Several AI-powered tools are available for effective social media monitoring, each offering unique features and capabilities:

Hootsuite Insights

- **Overview**: Hootsuite Insights uses AI to analyze social media conversations and provide insights into public sentiment and trends.
- **Features**: Real-time monitoring, sentiment analysis, trend identification, and comprehensive reporting.

Brandwatch

- **Overview**: Brandwatch offers advanced AI-driven analytics for social media listening and brand monitoring.
- **Features**: Sentiment analysis, image recognition, trend tracking, and influencer identification.

Sprout Social

- **Overview**: Sprout Social provides AI-powered tools for social media management and analytics.
- **Features**: Social listening, sentiment analysis, engagement tracking, and performance reporting.

Talkwalker

- **Overview**: Talkwalker uses AI to provide in-depth social media analytics and insights.
- **Features**: Social media monitoring, image and video recognition, trend analysis, and competitive benchmarking.

Mention

- **Overview**: Mention offers real-time monitoring and analysis of social media mentions and online content.
- **Features**: Sentiment analysis, keyword tracking, influencer identification, and comprehensive reporting.

4. Challenges and Considerations

While AI-driven social media monitoring offers significant benefits, it also presents several challenges:

Data Volume and Complexity: The sheer volume of social media data can be overwhelming. AI tools must efficiently handle and process large datasets to extract relevant information.

Accuracy and Bias: AI models can sometimes produce inaccurate results or exhibit biases based on the training data. Continuous refinement and validation are necessary to ensure accuracy and fairness.

Privacy Concerns: Social media monitoring must balance the need for intelligence with respect for user privacy and compliance with data protection regulations.

Contextual Understanding: AI tools may struggle with understanding the context and nuances of social media content, leading to potential misinterpretations.

5. Best Practices for Effective Social Media Monitoring

To maximize the benefits of AI-driven social media monitoring, organizations should follow these best practices:

Define Clear Objectives: Establish specific goals for social media monitoring, such as identifying emerging threats, managing brand reputation, or conducting market research.

Choose the Right Tools: Select AI tools that align with your objectives and offer the necessary features for effective monitoring and analysis.

Regularly Update Models: Continuously update and refine AI models to adapt to evolving trends, language, and user behavior.

Monitor and Validate: Regularly monitor the performance of AI tools and validate their outputs to ensure accuracy and reliability.

Ensure Compliance: Adhere to privacy regulations and ethical guidelines when collecting and analyzing social media data.

AI-driven social media monitoring provides powerful capabilities for extracting actionable insights from vast amounts of user-generated content. By leveraging techniques such as NLP, image recognition, and trend analysis, organizations can enhance their ability to detect threats, manage their brand reputation, and conduct market research. Despite challenges such as data volume, accuracy, and privacy concerns, implementing best practices and selecting the right tools can maximize the effectiveness of social media monitoring efforts. As social media continues to play a central role in information sharing and public discourse, AI will remain a critical component in understanding and leveraging this dynamic landscape.

5.2. AI in Analyzing Dark Web Activities

The dark web, a hidden part of the internet accessible only through specialized software like Tor, serves as a hub for various illicit activities, including illegal trade, cybercrime, and extremist discussions. Analyzing dark web activities is challenging due to its encrypted and anonymous nature, but AI technologies offer powerful tools to enhance detection, monitoring, and investigation. This section explores how AI is used to analyze dark web activities, the techniques and tools involved, and the challenges faced.

1. Importance of Analyzing Dark Web Activities

Analyzing dark web activities is crucial for several reasons:

Cybersecurity Threats: The dark web is a significant source of cyber threats, including the sale of stolen data, malware, and hacking services. Monitoring these activities helps in identifying and mitigating potential risks.

Illegal Trade and Trafficking: The dark web hosts illegal marketplaces for drugs, weapons, and human trafficking. Detecting and disrupting these activities is essential for law enforcement and regulatory agencies.

Extremist and Terrorist Activities: The dark web can be a platform for extremist groups and terrorists to communicate and plan operations. Monitoring these groups helps in preventing and responding to potential threats.

Fraud and Financial Crimes: Financial fraud, including identity theft and fraudulent transactions, often occurs on the dark web. Analyzing these activities aids in protecting individuals and organizations from financial loss.

2. Techniques for AI-Driven Dark Web Analysis

AI technologies enhance the ability to analyze and interpret dark web data through various techniques:

Natural Language Processing (NLP)

- **Text Analysis**: NLP algorithms process and analyze text data from dark web forums, marketplaces, and chat rooms. This includes detecting specific keywords, phrases, and topics related to illicit activities.
- **Sentiment Analysis**: AI models assess the sentiment of discussions to identify potential threats or indicators of malicious intent.
- **Entity Recognition**: NLP can identify and extract names, organizations, and other entities mentioned in dark web content, facilitating the tracking of individuals or groups involved in illicit activities.

Image and Video Analysis

- **Content Recognition**: AI-powered image and video recognition tools analyze visual content shared on dark web platforms, such as illegal product listings or propaganda materials.
- **Anomaly Detection**: These tools can identify unusual patterns or content that may indicate illegal activities, such as counterfeit goods or extremist imagery.

Network Analysis

- **Link Analysis**: AI tools map relationships between individuals, groups, and activities on the dark web. This helps in understanding networks and identifying key actors involved in illegal operations.
- **Social Network Analysis**: Analyzing social connections and interactions within dark web communities can reveal influential figures and their connections to illicit activities.

Behavioral Analysis

- **User Behavior**: AI models analyze user behavior patterns on dark web platforms, such as browsing habits and transaction history, to identify suspicious or potentially illegal activities.
- **Transaction Analysis**: AI tools track and analyze transactions on dark web marketplaces, including cryptocurrency exchanges, to detect fraudulent or illegal financial activities.

Anomaly Detection

- **Pattern Recognition**: AI algorithms identify anomalies in dark web data, such as sudden spikes in activity or unusual content, which may indicate emerging threats or new illegal activities.
- **Predictive Analytics**: Predictive models use historical data to forecast potential trends and emerging threats on the dark web.

3. Tools for AI-Driven Dark Web Analysis

Several AI-powered tools and platforms are designed specifically for analyzing dark web activities:

Darktrace

- **Overview**: Darktrace uses AI to detect and respond to anomalies and threats in real-time.
- **Features**: Automated threat detection, behavioral analysis, and real-time alerts for suspicious activities.

Palantir

- **Overview**: Palantir provides advanced analytics and data integration capabilities for dark web investigations.
- **Features**: Link analysis, network mapping, and advanced data visualization.

Cellebrite

- **Overview**: Cellebrite offers tools for digital forensics and dark web monitoring.

- **Features**: Data extraction, analysis of encrypted communications, and dark web data collection.

Recorded Future

- **Overview**: Recorded Future provides threat intelligence and analysis using AI and machine learning.
- **Features**: Real-time monitoring, sentiment analysis, and threat prediction.

Webhose

- **Overview**: Webhose offers dark web data extraction and analysis solutions.
- **Features**: Data aggregation, sentiment analysis, and content categorization.

4. Challenges and Considerations

Analyzing dark web activities using AI presents several challenges:

Anonymity and Encryption: The dark web's inherent anonymity and encryption make it difficult to trace and analyze user activities. AI tools must adapt to these challenges while maintaining effectiveness.

Data Volume and Quality: The sheer volume of data on the dark web can be overwhelming. Ensuring the quality and relevance of the data analyzed by AI tools is crucial for accurate insights.

False Positives and Bias: AI models may generate false positives or biased results based on training data. Continuous refinement and validation are necessary to minimize errors and ensure accurate detection.

Legal and Ethical Considerations: Monitoring and analyzing dark web activities must be conducted within legal and ethical boundaries. Ensuring compliance with privacy regulations and avoiding potential misuse of data are critical.

Adapting to Evolving Threats: The dark web is constantly evolving, with new platforms and technologies emerging. AI tools must be adaptable and updated regularly to address evolving threats and challenges.

5. Best Practices for Effective Dark Web Analysis

To maximize the effectiveness of AI-driven dark web analysis, organizations should follow these best practices:

Define Clear Objectives: Establish specific goals for dark web analysis, such as identifying threat actors, detecting illicit activities, or monitoring extremist groups.

Select the Right Tools: Choose AI tools that align with your objectives and offer the necessary features for effective dark web monitoring and analysis.

Regularly Update Models: Continuously update and refine AI models to adapt to new threats, trends, and changes in dark web platforms.

Ensure Data Quality: Validate and clean data to ensure accuracy and relevance in the analysis process.

Balance Privacy and Security: Adhere to legal and ethical guidelines while conducting dark web analysis to protect user privacy and comply with regulations.

AI-driven analysis of dark web activities provides valuable capabilities for detecting and understanding illicit activities hidden within this concealed part of the internet. By leveraging techniques such as NLP, image recognition, network analysis, and behavioral analysis, organizations can enhance their ability to monitor and respond to threats effectively. Despite challenges related to anonymity, data volume, and legal considerations, implementing best practices and using the right tools can significantly improve the effectiveness of dark web analysis and contribute to overall cybersecurity and investigative efforts.

5.3. Real-Time Data Collection and Analysis

Real-time data collection and analysis are pivotal in today's fast-paced digital landscape, where timely information can significantly impact decision-making and operational efficiency. The ability to collect and analyze data as events unfold allows organizations to respond swiftly to emerging threats, market changes, or operational issues. This section explores the methodologies, technologies, and best practices associated with real-time data collection and analysis, emphasizing the role of AI in enhancing these processes.

1. The Importance of Real-Time Data Collection and Analysis

Immediate Response: Real-time data enables organizations to react promptly to incidents, such as cybersecurity breaches, system failures, or customer complaints. This immediate response capability is crucial for mitigating risks and minimizing damage.

Enhanced Decision-Making: Timely insights derived from real-time data support informed decision-making. Whether it's adjusting marketing strategies based on current trends or making operational changes in response to real-time performance metrics, timely data is essential.

Competitive Advantage: Organizations that leverage real-time data gain a competitive edge by quickly adapting to market changes, identifying opportunities, and addressing challenges faster than competitors.

Operational Efficiency: Real-time monitoring of systems and processes helps in identifying inefficiencies, bottlenecks, or anomalies, allowing for prompt corrective actions and improving overall operational efficiency.

2. Techniques for Real-Time Data Collection

Data Streaming

- **Overview**: Data streaming involves continuous transmission of data from various sources, such as sensors, social media, or transactional systems. It allows for the real-time ingestion and processing of data.
- **Technologies**: Technologies such as Apache Kafka, Apache Flink, and AWS Kinesis enable scalable and efficient data streaming.

APIs and Webhooks

- **Overview**: APIs (Application Programming Interfaces) and webhooks facilitate the real-time exchange of data between systems. APIs allow applications to request data, while webhooks provide automatic notifications when specific events occur.
- **Applications**: APIs and webhooks are commonly used for integrating data from social media platforms, financial systems, or IoT devices.

Event-Driven Architecture

- **Overview**: Event-driven architecture (EDA) focuses on producing, detecting, and reacting to events in real time. It decouples systems and allows for asynchronous data processing.
- **Benefits**: EDA improves scalability and responsiveness by enabling systems to react to events as they occur rather than processing data in batches.

Real-Time Data Collection Tools

Examples: Tools such as Splunk, ElasticSearch, and Datadog offer capabilities for real-time data collection and monitoring across various systems and applications.

3. Techniques for Real-Time Data Analysis

Stream Processing

- **Overview**: Stream processing involves analyzing data in motion as it flows through a system. It enables real-time insights and decision-making based on live data.
- **Technologies**: Tools like Apache Storm, Apache Samza, and Google Cloud Dataflow support stream processing.

Real-Time Analytics Platforms

- **Overview**: Real-time analytics platforms aggregate and analyze data from multiple sources to provide immediate insights. These platforms often include features for visualization, alerting, and reporting.
- **Examples**: Platforms such as Tableau, Power BI, and Grafana offer real-time analytics capabilities with interactive dashboards and visualizations.

Machine Learning for Real-Time Analysis

- **Overview**: AI and machine learning models can analyze real-time data to identify patterns, anomalies, or trends. These models can be deployed to provide predictive analytics and automated decision-making.
- **Applications**: Machine learning models can be used for real-time fraud detection, predictive maintenance, and anomaly detection.

Edge Computing

- **Overview**: Edge computing involves processing data closer to its source, such as IoT devices or sensors, rather than sending it to a central server. This reduces latency and enables faster analysis.
- **Benefits**: Edge computing enhances real-time data processing by minimizing the delay associated with data transmission and central processing.

4. Tools and Technologies for Real-Time Data Collection and Analysis

Splunk

- **Overview**: Splunk provides real-time data collection, indexing, and analysis capabilities. It is widely used for monitoring IT systems, security events, and operational data.
- **Features**: Real-time search, alerting, visualization, and reporting.

Apache Kafka

- **Overview**: Apache Kafka is a distributed event streaming platform that handles real-time data feeds. It supports high-throughput data streaming and integration.
- **Features**: Real-time data ingestion, stream processing, and event sourcing.

AWS Kinesis

- **Overview**: AWS Kinesis offers services for real-time data streaming and processing. It enables the collection, processing, and analysis of data from various sources.
- **Features**: Real-time data streaming, analytics, and integration with other AWS services.

Elasticsearch

- **Overview**: Elasticsearch provides real-time search and analytics capabilities for large volumes of data. It is often used in conjunction with Logstash and Kibana (the ELK stack).
- **Features**: Full-text search, real-time data indexing, and analytics.

Datadog

- **Overview**: Datadog is a cloud-based monitoring and analytics platform that provides real-time visibility into applications and infrastructure.

- **Features**: Real-time metrics, log management, and performance monitoring.

5. Challenges and Considerations

Data Volume and Velocity: Handling large volumes of data streaming at high velocity can be challenging. Ensuring the scalability and performance of data collection and analysis systems is crucial.

Data Quality and Consistency: Real-time data collection requires high-quality and consistent data. Inaccurate or incomplete data can lead to incorrect insights and decisions.

Latency and Performance: Minimizing latency and optimizing performance are essential for effective real-time analysis. Ensuring that systems can handle high throughput and low latency is critical.

Integration with Existing Systems: Integrating real-time data collection and analysis with existing systems and workflows requires careful planning and implementation.

Security and Privacy: Ensuring the security and privacy of real-time data is vital. Implementing proper encryption, access controls, and compliance measures is necessary to protect sensitive information.

6. Best Practices for Real-Time Data Collection and Analysis

Define Clear Objectives: Establish specific goals for real-time data collection and analysis, such as improving operational efficiency, enhancing customer experience, or detecting threats.

Choose the Right Tools: Select tools and technologies that align with your objectives and support real-time data collection and analysis effectively.

Ensure Scalability: Design systems that can scale to handle increasing data volumes and maintain performance.

Optimize Performance: Continuously monitor and optimize system performance to minimize latency and ensure timely analysis.

Maintain Data Quality: Implement measures to ensure data accuracy, consistency, and reliability.

Implement Security Measures: Protect real-time data with appropriate security measures, including encryption, access controls, and compliance with regulations.

Real-time data collection and analysis are critical for responding to dynamic and fast-changing environments. By leveraging techniques such as data streaming, event-driven architecture, and AI-powered analytics, organizations can gain immediate insights and make informed decisions. Despite challenges related to data volume, latency, and security, implementing best practices and using the right tools can significantly enhance the effectiveness of real-time data analysis. As the demand for timely information grows, real-time data collection and analysis will continue to play a vital role in achieving operational excellence and maintaining a competitive edge.

5.4. Predictive Analytics for Cyber Threats

Predictive analytics is a powerful tool in the realm of cybersecurity, enabling organizations to anticipate and mitigate potential threats before they materialize. By leveraging historical data, statistical algorithms, and machine learning techniques, predictive analytics provides actionable insights into future risks and vulnerabilities. This section explores the methodologies, benefits, tools, and challenges associated with using predictive analytics for cyber threats.

1. The Importance of Predictive Analytics in Cybersecurity

Proactive Threat Detection: Predictive analytics helps identify potential threats before they escalate into actual security incidents. By analyzing historical data and trends, organizations can anticipate attacks and implement preventive measures.

Enhanced Risk Management: Predictive models assist in assessing and managing risks by providing insights into the likelihood and potential impact of different types of cyber threats. This enables better prioritization and resource allocation.

Improved Incident Response: Predictive analytics can forecast attack patterns and identify vulnerabilities, allowing security teams to develop more effective incident response plans and strategies.

Cost Savings: By preventing security incidents and minimizing damage, predictive analytics can lead to significant cost savings associated with data breaches, system downtimes, and recovery efforts.

2. Techniques for Predictive Analytics in Cybersecurity

Data Collection and Integration

- **Overview**: Collecting and integrating data from various sources, including network logs, security incidents, threat intelligence feeds, and user behavior, is crucial for building accurate predictive models.
- **Sources**: Common data sources include firewall logs, intrusion detection systems (IDS), antivirus software, and threat intelligence platforms.

Statistical Analysis

- **Overview**: Statistical techniques analyze historical data to identify patterns, trends, and correlations that can indicate potential future threats.
- **Techniques**: Techniques such as regression analysis, time series analysis, and clustering are used to identify patterns and predict future threat behaviors.

Machine Learning Models

- **Overview**: Machine learning algorithms are employed to create predictive models that can learn from historical data and make predictions about future threats.
- **Algorithms**: Common algorithms used in predictive analytics include decision trees, random forests, support vector machines, and neural networks.

Behavioral Analysis

- **Overview**: Analyzing user and network behavior helps in identifying deviations from normal patterns that could indicate potential security threats.
- **Techniques**: Behavioral analysis includes user behavior analytics (UBA) and network behavior analysis (NBA) to detect anomalies and predict potential attacks.

Threat Intelligence Integration

- **Overview**: Integrating threat intelligence feeds with predictive analytics enhances the ability to anticipate emerging threats and vulnerabilities.
- **Sources**: Threat intelligence sources include open-source intelligence (OSINT), commercial threat intelligence providers, and government agencies.

3. Tools for Predictive Analytics in Cybersecurity

Splunk Enterprise Security

- **Overview**: Splunk Enterprise Security provides predictive analytics capabilities for security monitoring and threat detection.
- **Features**: Real-time monitoring, correlation searches, anomaly detection, and predictive modeling.

IBM QRadar

- **Overview**: IBM QRadar offers advanced analytics for security information and event management (SIEM), including predictive analytics for threat detection.
- **Features**: Log and event data analysis, threat intelligence integration, and behavioral analytics.

Darktrace

- **Overview**: Darktrace uses AI and machine learning to provide predictive analytics for threat detection and response.
- **Features**: Anomaly detection, threat prediction, and real-time alerts.

Sumo Logic

- **Overview**: Sumo Logic provides cloud-native analytics for security and operations, including predictive analytics for identifying potential threats.
- **Features**: Real-time log analysis, machine learning insights, and threat detection.

Elastic Security

- **Overview**: Elastic Security offers predictive analytics capabilities for detecting and responding to cyber threats.
- **Features**: Threat hunting, anomaly detection, and machine learning models.

4. Challenges and Considerations

Data Quality and Quantity: The accuracy of predictive models depends on the quality and quantity of the data used. Incomplete or inaccurate data can lead to unreliable predictions.

Model Complexity and Interpretability: Complex machine learning models can be difficult to interpret, making it challenging to understand how predictions are made and to trust the results.

Evolving Threat Landscape: The rapidly changing nature of cyber threats requires continuous updates to predictive models and data sources to remain effective.

False Positives and Negatives: Predictive analytics may produce false positives (incorrectly predicting a threat) or false negatives (failing to predict an actual threat). Balancing sensitivity and specificity is crucial.

Integration with Existing Systems: Implementing predictive analytics requires integration with existing security infrastructure, which can be complex and resource-intensive.

5. Best Practices for Implementing Predictive Analytics for Cyber Threats

Define Clear Objectives: Establish specific goals for predictive analytics, such as detecting specific types of threats, improving response times, or enhancing risk management.

Ensure Data Quality: Invest in data collection and integration processes to ensure that the data used for predictive modeling is accurate, complete, and relevant.

Select the Right Tools: Choose predictive analytics tools that align with your organization's needs and provide the necessary features for effective threat detection and analysis.

Continuously Update Models: Regularly update and refine predictive models to adapt to new threats, changes in attack patterns, and advancements in technology.

Balance Sensitivity and Specificity: Fine-tune predictive models to minimize false positives and false negatives, ensuring accurate and actionable predictions.

Integrate with Incident Response: Ensure that predictive analytics insights are integrated into incident response plans and processes to facilitate timely and effective actions.

Predictive analytics offers significant advantages in the field of cybersecurity by enabling organizations to anticipate and address potential threats before they materialize. Through techniques such as statistical analysis, machine learning, and behavioral analysis, predictive analytics provides valuable insights into future risks and vulnerabilities. Despite challenges related to data quality, model complexity, and evolving threats, implementing best practices and using the right tools can enhance the effectiveness of predictive analytics in cyber threat detection and management. As cyber threats continue to evolve, predictive analytics will play a crucial role in staying ahead of potential risks and safeguarding organizational assets.

5.5. AI in Identifying Emerging Threat Patterns

In the rapidly evolving landscape of cybersecurity, identifying emerging threat patterns is crucial for preemptively addressing potential risks and vulnerabilities. Traditional methods of threat detection often fall short in the face of sophisticated and novel attack strategies. Artificial Intelligence (AI) offers a transformative approach by leveraging advanced algorithms and data analysis techniques to recognize and predict emerging threat patterns before they cause significant damage. This section explores how AI is used to identify emerging threat patterns, including the methodologies, tools, benefits, and challenges associated with this approach.

1. The Need for Identifying Emerging Threat Patterns

Proactive Defense: Identifying emerging threat patterns allows organizations to adopt a proactive stance in cybersecurity. By understanding and anticipating new attack strategies, security teams can implement defensive measures before an attack occurs.

Adapting to Evolving Threats: Cyber threats are constantly evolving, with attackers developing new techniques and exploiting novel vulnerabilities. AI helps in adapting to these changes by continuously analyzing and learning from new data.

Reducing Response Time: Early identification of emerging threat patterns reduces the time needed to detect and respond to security incidents, thereby minimizing potential damage and improving overall incident response.

Resource Optimization: Recognizing emerging threats enables better allocation of resources by focusing on high-risk areas and optimizing security measures based on the latest threat intelligence.

2. AI Techniques for Identifying Emerging Threat Patterns

Machine Learning Algorithms

- **Overview**: Machine learning algorithms analyze large volumes of data to identify patterns and anomalies that may indicate emerging threats. These algorithms learn from historical data and adapt to new patterns over time.
- **Algorithms**: Commonly used algorithms include clustering (e.g., K-means), classification (e.g., decision trees, random forests), and anomaly detection (e.g., isolation forests, one-class SVM).

Natural Language Processing (NLP)

- **Overview**: NLP techniques analyze textual data from sources such as threat intelligence reports, forums, and social media to identify new threat patterns and trends.
- **Applications**: NLP can detect emerging threat discussions, new malware names, and attack methods by analyzing language and sentiment.

Behavioral Analysis

- **Overview**: AI models analyze user and network behavior to detect deviations from normal patterns that could signify emerging threats.
- **Techniques**: Behavioral analysis includes monitoring network traffic, user activity, and application usage to identify anomalies that may indicate new attack vectors.

Pattern Recognition

- **Overview**: AI systems use pattern recognition techniques to identify recurring attack patterns and variations that could signify the emergence of new threats.
- **Methods**: Pattern recognition methods include statistical pattern recognition, deep learning-based feature extraction, and rule-based systems.

Predictive Modeling

- **Overview**: Predictive models use historical data and machine learning to forecast potential future threats based on emerging patterns and trends.
- **Applications**: Predictive modeling can identify potential new attack methods, vulnerabilities, and targets by analyzing historical threat data and trends.

3. Tools and Platforms for AI-Driven Threat Pattern Identification

Darktrace

- **Overview**: Darktrace utilizes AI and machine learning to detect and respond to emerging threats by analyzing network and user behavior.
- **Features**: Anomaly detection, real-time threat analysis, and adaptive learning.

CrowdStrike Falcon

- **Overview**: CrowdStrike Falcon employs AI-driven endpoint protection to identify and respond to new and emerging threats.
- **Features**: Behavioral analysis, machine learning detection, and threat intelligence integration.

IBM QRadar

- **Overview**: IBM QRadar integrates AI and machine learning for advanced threat detection and pattern recognition.
- **Features**: Real-time analytics, anomaly detection, and predictive threat intelligence.

Sumo Logic

- **Overview**: Sumo Logic provides cloud-native analytics with AI capabilities to identify emerging threat patterns and trends.
- **Features**: Real-time log analysis, machine learning insights, and threat detection.

Elastic Security

- **Overview**: Elastic Security uses AI and machine learning to detect and analyze emerging threat patterns in real-time.
- **Features**: Threat hunting, anomaly detection, and machine learning-based insights.

4. Challenges and Considerations

Data Quality and Integration: Effective AI-driven threat pattern identification requires high-quality and integrated data from diverse sources. Incomplete or inaccurate data can hinder the accuracy of threat detection.

False Positives and Negatives: AI models may produce false positives (incorrectly identifying benign activity as a threat) or false negatives (failing to detect actual threats). Balancing sensitivity and specificity is crucial.

Adaptability to New Threats: As attackers continually evolve their methods, AI systems must be adaptable and continuously updated to recognize new and emerging threat patterns.

Complexity of AI Models: Some AI models, especially deep learning models, can be complex and difficult to interpret. Understanding how predictions are made and ensuring transparency is important for trust and validation.

Resource Intensive: Implementing AI-driven threat detection systems can be resource-intensive, requiring significant computational power, data storage, and expertise.

5. Best Practices for Using AI to Identify Emerging Threat Patterns

Leverage Diverse Data Sources: Integrate data from multiple sources, including network logs, threat intelligence feeds, and user behavior data, to enhance the accuracy of threat pattern identification.

Continuously Update Models: Regularly update and refine AI models to incorporate new threat data and adapt to evolving attack techniques and patterns.

Monitor and Evaluate Performance: Continuously monitor the performance of AI-driven threat detection systems, evaluating their effectiveness and adjusting parameters to reduce false positives and negatives.

Implement Hybrid Approaches: Combine AI-driven methods with traditional threat detection approaches to create a more comprehensive and effective security strategy.

Ensure Transparency and Explainability: Use AI models that offer transparency and explainability, allowing security teams to understand how predictions are made and build trust in the system.

Invest in Training and Expertise: Provide training for security teams to effectively use and interpret AI-driven threat detection tools, ensuring they can leverage the insights provided to enhance security measures.

AI plays a critical role in identifying emerging threat patterns by leveraging advanced techniques such as machine learning, natural language processing, and behavioral analysis. These capabilities enable organizations to anticipate and respond to new and evolving threats more effectively. Despite challenges related to data quality, model complexity, and resource requirements, implementing best practices and using the right tools can significantly enhance the ability to detect and address emerging cybersecurity threats. As the threat landscape continues to evolve, AI-driven threat pattern identification will remain a vital component of a proactive and adaptive cybersecurity strategy.

Chapter 6: AI-Driven Automation in Cyber Investigations

Chapter 6, "AI-Driven Automation in Cyber Investigations," explores the transformative impact of Artificial Intelligence (AI) on automating key aspects of cyber investigations. This chapter delves into how AI technologies streamline processes such as data collection, analysis, and threat detection, significantly reducing the time and effort required for these tasks. By automating repetitive and data-intensive activities, AI enhances the efficiency and accuracy of investigations while allowing human analysts to focus on more complex and strategic aspects. The chapter also addresses the challenges and considerations associated with integrating AI-driven automation into existing workflows, highlighting both the benefits and the need for balanced human oversight.

6.1. Automating Data Collection with AI

Automating data collection with AI is revolutionizing the way organizations gather, process, and analyze information. Traditional methods of data collection can be labor-intensive and prone to errors, but AI-driven automation streamlines these processes, enhancing efficiency, accuracy, and scalability. This section explores the principles, methodologies, benefits, and challenges of using AI for automating data collection.

1. The Importance of Automating Data Collection

Efficiency and Speed: Automated data collection speeds up the process of gathering information from various sources, reducing the time required compared to manual methods. This is particularly important in fast-paced environments where timely data is crucial.

Scalability: AI-driven automation allows organizations to scale their data collection efforts without a proportional increase in resources. This is essential for handling large volumes of data from diverse sources.

Accuracy and Consistency: Automation reduces human error and ensures consistent data collection practices, leading to more reliable and accurate datasets.

Resource Optimization: By automating routine data collection tasks, organizations can reallocate human resources to more strategic activities, such as data analysis and decision-making.

Real-Time Data Collection: Automated systems can collect data in real time, providing up-to-date information that is critical for dynamic and time-sensitive decision-making.

2. AI Techniques for Automating Data Collection

Web Scraping

- **Overview**: Web scraping involves using AI algorithms to extract data from websites and online sources. This technique is useful for gathering information from publicly available web pages.
- **Tools**: AI-powered web scraping tools like Beautiful Soup, Scrapy, and Octoparse automate the extraction of data from various web sources.

Natural Language Processing (NLP)

- **Overview**: NLP techniques enable AI systems to process and extract relevant information from textual data, such as news articles, reports, and social media posts.
- **Applications**: NLP can be used to automatically summarize text, extract key entities and relationships, and categorize content.

Robotic Process Automation (RPA)

- **Overview**: RPA uses AI-driven robots or software bots to automate repetitive tasks and data collection processes across different systems and applications.
- **Applications**: RPA can automate data entry, form filling, and information retrieval from various sources.

Data Extraction from APIs

- **Overview**: Many online platforms provide APIs (Application Programming Interfaces) that allow for automated data retrieval. AI can be used to interact with these APIs and collect data efficiently.
- **Examples**: Collecting data from social media APIs (e.g., Twitter API), financial market APIs, and weather data APIs.

Image and Video Analysis

- **Overview**: AI algorithms can analyze images and videos to extract data and insights. Techniques such as computer vision and image recognition enable automated data collection from visual media.
- **Applications**: Image and video analysis can be used for monitoring surveillance footage, analyzing product images, and extracting information from visual content.

3. Tools and Platforms for AI-Driven Data Collection

Beautiful Soup

- **Overview**: Beautiful Soup is a Python library for web scraping that simplifies the process of extracting data from HTML and XML files.
- **Features**: Parsing HTML/XML, searching for specific elements, and extracting data.

Scrapy

- **Overview**: Scrapy is an open-source web crawling framework that allows for the automated extraction of data from websites.
- **Features**: Web crawling, data extraction, and data storage.

Octoparse

- **Overview**: Octoparse is a no-code web scraping tool that provides a user-friendly interface for automated data extraction from websites.
- **Features**: Point-and-click interface, scheduled scraping, and data export.

Amazon Textract

- **Overview**: Amazon Textract is a machine learning service that automatically extracts text, forms, and tables from scanned documents.
- **Features**: Optical character recognition (OCR), form extraction, and structured data extraction.

Google Cloud Vision

- **Overview**: Google Cloud Vision provides AI-powered image analysis capabilities, including object detection, text extraction, and label recognition.
- **Features**: Image recognition, text extraction, and visual content analysis.

UiPath

- **Overview**: UiPath is a leading RPA platform that enables automation of repetitive tasks and processes, including data collection from various sources.
- **Features**: Workflow automation, data extraction, and process integration.

4. Challenges and Considerations

Data Privacy and Compliance: Automated data collection must adhere to data privacy regulations and compliance standards, such as GDPR and CCPA. Ensuring that data collection practices respect user privacy and legal requirements is crucial.

Data Quality and Integrity: Automated systems may sometimes collect incomplete or inaccurate data. Ensuring data quality through validation and verification processes is essential.

Complexity of Implementation: Setting up and configuring AI-driven data collection systems can be complex and may require specialized expertise and resources.

Handling Unstructured Data: Many sources of data, such as social media posts and news articles, are unstructured and require advanced NLP techniques for meaningful extraction and analysis.

Integration with Existing Systems: Automated data collection systems need to be integrated with existing IT infrastructure and data processing systems to ensure seamless data flow and utilization.

5. Best Practices for Automating Data Collection with AI

Define Clear Objectives: Establish specific goals for automated data collection, such as improving data accuracy, increasing collection speed, or expanding data sources.

Select the Right Tools: Choose AI tools and platforms that align with your data collection needs and provide the necessary features for effective automation.

Ensure Data Quality: Implement processes to validate and verify the accuracy and completeness of collected data, addressing any issues promptly.

Respect Privacy and Compliance: Adhere to data privacy regulations and ensure that automated data collection practices comply with relevant legal and ethical standards.

Monitor and Optimize: Continuously monitor the performance of automated data collection systems and optimize them based on feedback and evolving requirements.

Invest in Training and Support: Provide training for staff to effectively use and manage AI-driven data collection tools, and seek support from vendors as needed.

Automating data collection with AI offers significant advantages in terms of efficiency, accuracy, and scalability. By leveraging techniques such as web scraping, NLP, RPA, and image analysis, organizations can streamline their data collection processes and gain valuable insights in real time. Despite challenges related to data privacy, quality, and system complexity, implementing best practices and using the right tools can enhance the effectiveness of AI-driven data collection. As data becomes increasingly central to decision-making and operational success, automation will play a crucial role in managing and harnessing this valuable resource.

6.2. Streamlining Data Analysis Through AI

In the modern data-driven world, the sheer volume and complexity of data can overwhelm traditional analysis methods. AI technologies are transforming data analysis by providing advanced tools and techniques that streamline the process, enhance accuracy, and uncover actionable insights more efficiently. This section explores how AI is used to streamline data analysis, covering methodologies, benefits, tools, and challenges associated with this approach.

1. The Need for AI in Data Analysis

Handling Large Volumes of Data: AI excels at processing and analyzing vast amounts of data quickly, making it essential for organizations dealing with big data. Traditional methods often struggle with the scale and speed required for timely analysis.

Extracting Valuable Insights: AI-driven data analysis can uncover patterns, trends, and correlations that may be missed by manual analysis. This enables organizations to make more informed decisions based on comprehensive data insights.

Improving Accuracy and Reducing Errors: AI reduces human error and bias in data analysis, leading to more accurate and reliable results. Automated algorithms consistently apply the same criteria and methodologies, enhancing the consistency of analyses.

Real-Time Analysis: AI enables real-time data analysis, allowing organizations to respond swiftly to emerging trends, anomalies, or issues. This is crucial for dynamic environments where timely decisions are necessary.

Enhancing Decision-Making: By automating complex analytical tasks, AI helps decision-makers focus on strategic actions rather than being bogged down by data processing tasks.

2. AI Techniques for Streamlining Data Analysis

Machine Learning Algorithms

- **Overview**: Machine learning (ML) algorithms are used to analyze data and identify patterns without explicit programming. They learn from historical data to make predictions or decisions based on new data.
- **Techniques**: Common ML techniques include supervised learning (e.g., regression, classification), unsupervised learning (e.g., clustering, dimensionality reduction), and reinforcement learning.

Natural Language Processing (NLP)

- **Overview**: NLP techniques analyze and interpret human language data, enabling AI systems to understand and process text-based information.
- **Applications**: NLP is used for sentiment analysis, topic modeling, text summarization, and extracting insights from unstructured data sources like social media and customer feedback.

Data Mining

- **Overview**: Data mining involves discovering patterns and relationships in large datasets through statistical and computational techniques. AI enhances data mining by automating the discovery process and improving accuracy.
- **Techniques**: Techniques include association rule mining, sequence mining, and anomaly detection.

Predictive Analytics

- **Overview**: Predictive analytics uses historical data and AI models to forecast future trends and behaviors. This technique helps in anticipating potential outcomes and guiding decision-making.
- **Applications**: Predictive analytics is used for demand forecasting, risk management, and customer behavior analysis.

Deep Learning

- **Overview**: Deep learning, a subset of machine learning, uses neural networks with multiple layers to model complex data representations. It is particularly effective for tasks such as image and speech recognition.
- **Applications**: Deep learning is used for advanced pattern recognition, natural language understanding, and automated data interpretation.

3. Tools and Platforms for AI-Driven Data Analysis

Google BigQuery

- **Overview**: Google BigQuery is a fully-managed, serverless data warehouse that allows for fast SQL queries using machine learning models for advanced analytics.
- **Features**: Real-time data analysis, integration with Google Cloud AI, and support for large-scale data processing.

Microsoft Azure Machine Learning

- **Overview**: Microsoft Azure Machine Learning provides a suite of tools for building, training, and deploying machine learning models to analyze data.
- **Features**: Automated machine learning, data preparation, and model management.

IBM Watson Analytics

- **Overview**: IBM Watson Analytics offers AI-driven data analysis and visualization tools that help users uncover insights from their data.
- **Features**: Natural language queries, automated data exploration, and predictive analytics.

Tableau with Einstein Analytics

- **Overview**: Tableau integrates with Einstein Analytics to provide advanced data analysis and visualization capabilities powered by AI.
- **Features**: Predictive analytics, automated insights, and interactive dashboards.

RapidMiner

- **Overview**: RapidMiner is a data science platform that enables users to build, deploy, and manage AI models for data analysis.
- **Features**: Data preparation, machine learning, and model deployment.

4. Challenges and Considerations

Data Quality and Preprocessing: High-quality data is essential for accurate AI-driven analysis. Data preprocessing steps, such as cleaning and normalization, are critical for ensuring reliable results.

Model Interpretability: Some AI models, particularly deep learning models, can be complex and difficult to interpret. Ensuring that models provide explainable results is important for trust and decision-making.

Integration with Existing Systems: AI-driven data analysis tools must be integrated with existing IT infrastructure and data systems, which can be challenging and require careful planning.

Resource and Expertise Requirements: Implementing AI-driven data analysis requires specialized skills and resources. Organizations may need to invest in training and hire experts to effectively utilize these tools.

Ethical and Privacy Concerns: Handling sensitive data requires adherence to ethical guidelines and privacy regulations. Ensuring that AI analysis practices respect user privacy and data protection laws is crucial.

5. Best Practices for Streamlining Data Analysis with AI

Define Clear Objectives: Establish specific goals for AI-driven data analysis, such as improving decision-making, increasing efficiency, or identifying new trends.

Choose the Right Tools: Select AI tools and platforms that align with your data analysis needs and provide the necessary features for effective analysis.

Ensure Data Quality: Invest in data cleaning and preprocessing to ensure that the data used for analysis is accurate and reliable.

Monitor and Validate Results: Regularly monitor the performance of AI models and validate their results to ensure that they are producing accurate and actionable insights.

Promote Transparency and Explainability: Use AI models that offer transparency and explainability to help users understand how decisions are made and build trust in the system.

Invest in Training and Support: Provide training for staff to effectively use AI-driven data analysis tools and seek support from vendors as needed.

AI is significantly enhancing the efficiency and effectiveness of data analysis by automating complex tasks, uncovering valuable insights, and handling large volumes of data. Techniques such as machine learning, NLP, data mining, and deep learning are streamlining data analysis processes, enabling organizations to make more informed decisions and respond swiftly to emerging trends. Despite challenges related to data quality, model interpretability, and resource requirements, implementing best practices and utilizing the right tools can optimize AI-driven data analysis. As data continues to play a central role in decision-making, AI will be instrumental in transforming how organizations analyze and leverage their data assets.

6.3. Balancing Automation with Human Oversight

In the realm of data analysis and cybersecurity, striking the right balance between automation and human oversight is crucial for optimizing performance and ensuring effective outcomes. While AI-driven automation offers significant benefits in terms of efficiency, accuracy, and scalability, human oversight remains essential for addressing complex scenarios, validating results, and making nuanced decisions. This section explores the importance of balancing automation with human oversight, outlining methodologies, benefits, challenges, and best practices.

1. The Importance of Balancing Automation with Human Oversight

Enhancing Accuracy and Reliability: Automated systems can process data at scale and speed but may produce errors or overlook nuances. Human oversight helps verify and validate results, ensuring that automated outputs are accurate and reliable.

Handling Complex and Ambiguous Situations: AI systems are powerful but can struggle with complex or ambiguous situations that require context, intuition, and critical thinking. Human oversight is crucial for addressing these complexities and making informed decisions.

Ensuring Ethical and Regulatory Compliance: Automated systems may inadvertently violate ethical guidelines or regulatory requirements. Human oversight ensures that automated processes adhere to legal and ethical standards.

Improving System Adaptability: While AI systems can adapt to new data, they may not always adjust effectively to sudden changes or novel scenarios. Human oversight provides an additional layer of adaptability and responsiveness.

Providing Context and Judgment: Human judgment is essential for interpreting results in context and considering factors that automated systems may not fully account for. This helps in making more nuanced and context-aware decisions.

2. Methodologies for Balancing Automation and Human Oversight

Hybrid Decision-Making Models

- **Overview**: Hybrid decision-making models combine automated analysis with human review to leverage the strengths of both approaches. AI handles routine tasks and data processing, while humans provide oversight and make final decisions.
- **Applications**: These models are used in areas such as fraud detection, where AI identifies potential fraud cases, and human analysts review and confirm suspicious activities.

Human-in-the-Loop (HITL) Systems

- **Overview**: Human-in-the-loop systems integrate human input into automated processes, allowing for continuous oversight and intervention. This approach ensures that human expertise is incorporated at critical stages.
- **Applications**: HITL systems are used in machine learning model training, where human feedback is used to refine algorithms and improve accuracy.

Automated Alerts and Human Review

- **Overview**: Automated systems generate alerts based on predefined criteria, which are then reviewed by human analysts. This approach helps prioritize tasks and ensures that critical issues are addressed promptly.
- **Applications**: Automated threat detection systems generate alerts for potential security incidents, which are reviewed by cybersecurity professionals to determine the appropriate response.

Continuous Monitoring and Feedback

- **Overview**: Continuous monitoring involves regularly evaluating the performance of automated systems and providing feedback for improvements. This iterative process helps refine algorithms and enhance overall effectiveness.
- **Applications**: Continuous monitoring is used in AI-driven data analysis to track the accuracy of predictions and adjust models based on new data and insights.

3. Benefits of Balancing Automation with Human Oversight

Increased Accuracy: Combining automated processing with human review enhances the overall accuracy of results by addressing potential errors and validating outputs.

Enhanced Flexibility: Human oversight provides the flexibility to adapt to complex and evolving situations that automated systems may struggle with, improving overall responsiveness.

Reduced Risk of Bias: Automated systems may inadvertently perpetuate biases present in the data. Human oversight helps identify and mitigate biases, ensuring fair and unbiased outcomes.

Improved Decision-Making: Balancing automation with human judgment leads to more informed and context-aware decision-making, enhancing the quality of outcomes.

Greater Compliance and Ethics: Human oversight ensures that automated processes adhere to ethical standards and regulatory requirements, reducing the risk of non-compliance.

4. Challenges of Balancing Automation with Human Oversight

Resource Allocation: Maintaining human oversight requires additional resources, including personnel and time. Balancing these resources with automation can be challenging, particularly in resource-constrained environments.

Complexity of Integration: Integrating automated systems with human oversight processes can be complex, requiring careful coordination and communication between automated tools and human reviewers.

Over-Reliance on Automation: There is a risk of over-relying on automation, leading to complacency and reduced attention to critical oversight tasks. Ensuring a balanced approach is essential to avoid this pitfall.

Training and Expertise: Effective oversight requires skilled personnel with the expertise to interpret automated results and make informed decisions. Training and maintaining expertise can be challenging.

Communication and Coordination: Ensuring effective communication and coordination between automated systems and human reviewers is crucial for maintaining oversight and achieving desired outcomes.

5. Best Practices for Balancing Automation and Human Oversight

Define Clear Roles and Responsibilities: Establish clear roles and responsibilities for both automated systems and human reviewers to ensure effective collaboration and oversight.

Implement Robust Validation Processes: Develop validation processes to review and verify automated outputs, ensuring accuracy and reliability in decision-making.

Provide Ongoing Training and Support: Offer regular training and support for personnel involved in oversight to ensure they are equipped with the necessary skills and knowledge.

Monitor System Performance: Continuously monitor the performance of automated systems and human oversight processes to identify areas for improvement and address any issues promptly.

Foster Collaboration: Encourage collaboration between automated systems and human reviewers to leverage the strengths of both approaches and enhance overall effectiveness.

Ensure Transparency: Maintain transparency in how automated systems operate and how decisions are made, ensuring that human reviewers have a clear understanding of the underlying processes and criteria.

Balancing automation with human oversight is essential for optimizing the performance and effectiveness of data analysis and cybersecurity processes. While AI-driven automation enhances efficiency and scalability, human oversight provides critical validation, context, and decision-making capabilities. By implementing hybrid decision-making models, human-in-the-loop systems, and continuous monitoring practices, organizations can achieve a balanced approach that leverages the strengths of both automation and human judgment. Despite challenges related to resource allocation, integration complexity, and training, adopting best practices and fostering effective collaboration can ensure that automation and oversight work together to deliver accurate, reliable, and context-aware outcomes.

6.4. The Role of AI in Speeding Up Investigations

In the context of investigations—whether in cybersecurity, law enforcement, or corporate settings—speed and efficiency are paramount. AI technologies play a crucial role in accelerating investigations by automating complex tasks, analyzing large volumes of data, and providing actionable insights. This section explores how AI contributes to speeding up investigations, highlighting its methodologies, benefits, tools, and challenges.

1. The Need for Speed in Investigations

Timeliness: In investigations, timely access to information and insights can be critical. Rapid responses can prevent further damage, mitigate risks, and lead to quicker resolutions.

Volume of Data: Modern investigations often involve vast amounts of data from various sources, such as digital records, communications, and sensor data. AI can process and analyze this data more quickly than traditional methods.

Complexity: Investigations can be complex, involving intricate patterns, relationships, and anomalies. AI's ability to handle complexity helps in uncovering hidden connections and insights.

Resource Constraints: Investigative teams may have limited resources and personnel. AI can help optimize the use of available resources by automating routine tasks and focusing human efforts on critical areas.

2. AI Techniques for Speeding Up Investigations

Automated Data Collection

- **Overview**: AI-powered tools automate the collection of data from various sources, including websites, databases, and social media platforms. This speeds up the process of gathering information required for investigations.
- **Applications**: Automated web scraping, API integration, and data mining are used to gather relevant data efficiently.

Natural Language Processing (NLP)

- **Overview**: NLP techniques enable AI systems to analyze and understand text data, including emails, reports, and social media posts. This speeds up the process of extracting relevant information and identifying key insights.
- **Applications**: NLP is used for entity extraction, sentiment analysis, and topic modeling to quickly identify relevant content.

Machine Learning and Predictive Analytics

- **Overview**: Machine learning algorithms can analyze historical data to predict future trends, identify patterns, and make recommendations. Predictive analytics helps in anticipating potential outcomes and guiding investigative strategies.
- **Applications**: Machine learning models can predict potential risks, identify emerging threats, and suggest investigative leads based on past data.

Pattern Recognition and Anomaly Detection

- **Overview**: AI algorithms are capable of recognizing patterns and detecting anomalies in large datasets. This helps in identifying unusual activities or behaviors that may be indicative of criminal or malicious activity.
- **Applications**: Pattern recognition is used in fraud detection, cyber threat analysis, and behavioral analysis to uncover suspicious activities.

Image and Video Analysis

- **Overview:** AI-driven image and video analysis tools can process and analyze visual data to extract information and identify objects, faces, and activities. This speeds up the review of surveillance footage and other visual evidence.
- **Applications:** AI is used for facial recognition, object detection, and video summarization to streamline the review of visual evidence.

3. Tools and Platforms for AI-Driven Investigations

Palantir

- **Overview:** Palantir is a data analytics platform that enables users to integrate, analyze, and visualize large volumes of data. It supports investigative efforts by providing advanced analytics and visualization tools.
- **Features:** Data integration, pattern recognition, and investigative collaboration tools.

IBM i2 Analyst's Notebook

- **Overview:** IBM i2 Analyst's Notebook is a visual analysis tool that helps investigators identify patterns, relationships, and trends in complex data sets.
- **Features:** Link analysis, visualization, and reporting tools.

Cortex XDR by Palo Alto Networks

- **Overview:** Cortex XDR is a cybersecurity platform that uses AI to detect and respond to threats by analyzing data across endpoints, networks, and cloud environments.
- **Features:** Threat detection, automated response, and analytics.

Microsoft Azure Sentinel

- **Overview:** Microsoft Azure Sentinel is a cloud-native SIEM (Security Information and Event Management) solution that uses AI and machine learning to provide advanced threat detection and investigation capabilities.
- **Features:** Security analytics, incident response, and integration with other security tools.

Exabeam

- **Overview**: Exabeam is a security analytics platform that leverages machine learning to detect and investigate security incidents. It automates the process of identifying and responding to threats.
- **Features**: Behavioral analytics, threat detection, and automated investigations.

4. Benefits of AI in Speeding Up Investigations

Increased Efficiency: AI automates time-consuming tasks, such as data collection and analysis, significantly speeding up investigative processes.

Enhanced Accuracy: AI algorithms reduce human error and bias, providing more accurate and reliable results in investigations.

Faster Decision-Making: AI provides rapid insights and recommendations, enabling investigators to make quicker decisions and take timely actions.

Improved Resource Utilization: By automating routine tasks, AI allows investigators to focus on higher-priority activities and strategic decision-making.

Broader Data Analysis: AI can analyze large and diverse datasets, uncovering insights and patterns that may be missed through manual analysis.

5. Challenges and Considerations

Data Privacy and Security: Handling sensitive data requires strict adherence to privacy and security regulations. Ensuring that AI systems protect data and comply with legal requirements is crucial.

Quality of Data: AI systems rely on high-quality data for accurate analysis. Poor data quality can lead to incorrect conclusions and undermine the effectiveness of automated tools.

Integration with Existing Systems: Integrating AI tools with existing investigative systems and workflows can be complex and may require careful planning and coordination.

Interpretability of AI Results: Some AI models, especially deep learning models, can be complex and difficult to interpret. Ensuring that results are understandable and actionable is important for effective use.

Ethical Considerations: The use of AI in investigations must consider ethical implications, including the potential for bias, fairness, and transparency in decision-making processes.

6. Best Practices for Leveraging AI in Investigations

Define Clear Objectives: Establish specific goals for using AI in investigations, such as improving speed, accuracy, or scope of analysis.

Select Appropriate Tools: Choose AI tools and platforms that align with your investigative needs and provide the necessary features for effective analysis.

Ensure Data Quality and Security: Maintain high standards for data quality and implement robust security measures to protect sensitive information.

Provide Training and Support: Offer training for investigators to effectively use AI tools and interpret results, and provide ongoing support to address any issues.

Monitor and Evaluate Performance: Regularly monitor the performance of AI systems and evaluate their effectiveness in speeding up investigations. Adjust strategies and tools based on feedback and performance metrics.

Balance Automation with Human Oversight: Ensure that AI-driven automation is complemented by human oversight to validate results, interpret complex situations, and make nuanced decisions.

AI plays a transformative role in speeding up investigations by automating data collection and analysis, enhancing accuracy, and providing timely insights. Techniques such as automated data collection, NLP, machine learning, and image analysis contribute to more efficient and effective investigative processes. Despite challenges related to data privacy, integration, and interpretability, leveraging AI tools can significantly improve the speed and quality of investigations. By implementing best practices and balancing automation with human oversight, organizations can optimize their investigative efforts and achieve better outcomes in a timely manner.

6.5. Challenges in Implementing AI-Driven Automation

Implementing AI-driven automation in various domains, including cybersecurity, data analysis, and investigative processes, can offer significant advantages in terms of efficiency, accuracy, and scalability. However, the adoption of AI-driven automation also comes with its own set of challenges. This section explores these challenges, offering insights into the complexities and considerations involved in successfully integrating AI-driven automation into existing systems and workflows.

1. Data Quality and Availability

Data Integrity: AI systems require high-quality data to function effectively. Inaccurate, incomplete, or outdated data can lead to erroneous results and undermine the reliability of automated processes.

Data Volume: Managing and processing large volumes of data can be challenging. Ensuring that AI systems have access to sufficient data for training and analysis while handling data scalability issues is crucial.

Data Integration: Integrating data from disparate sources can be complex. Ensuring that data is consistent, compatible, and formatted correctly for use in AI models requires careful planning and execution.

Data Privacy and Security: Protecting sensitive data and complying with privacy regulations is essential. AI systems must be designed to handle data securely and adhere to relevant legal and ethical standards.

2. Algorithmic Bias and Fairness

Bias in Data: AI systems can inherit and perpetuate biases present in the training data. This can lead to unfair or discriminatory outcomes, particularly if the data reflects historical inequalities or stereotypes.

Bias in Algorithms: Even with unbiased data, the algorithms themselves can introduce biases through their design or implementation. Ensuring that algorithms are fair and transparent is a key challenge.

Mitigation Strategies: Identifying and mitigating biases in AI systems requires ongoing monitoring and evaluation. Implementing strategies to detect and address bias is essential for maintaining fairness and equity.

3. System Integration and Compatibility

Integration Complexity: Integrating AI-driven automation with existing systems and workflows can be complex. Ensuring seamless compatibility and interoperability between new AI tools and legacy systems is a significant challenge.

Infrastructure Requirements: AI systems often require specialized infrastructure, including computing power and storage. Ensuring that the necessary infrastructure is in place and can support AI-driven automation is crucial.

Change Management: Implementing AI-driven automation may require changes to existing processes and workflows. Managing these changes and ensuring that staff are trained and prepared for new systems is essential.

4. Interpretability and Transparency

Complexity of AI Models: Some AI models, particularly deep learning models, can be complex and difficult to interpret. Ensuring that the results and decisions made by AI systems are understandable and actionable is important for trust and accountability.

Explainability: Providing explanations for AI-driven decisions and recommendations helps users understand the rationale behind them. Developing methods for explainable AI is a key challenge in maintaining transparency.

User Trust: Building and maintaining trust in AI systems requires transparency and clear communication about how the systems operate and make decisions. Users must have confidence in the reliability and fairness of the AI-driven automation.

5. Cost and Resource Implications

Initial Investment: Implementing AI-driven automation can require significant initial investment in technology, infrastructure, and expertise. Evaluating the cost-benefit ratio and securing funding for these investments is a challenge.

Ongoing Maintenance: AI systems require ongoing maintenance, including updates, monitoring, and tuning. Managing the costs associated with maintaining and supporting AI-driven automation is essential for long-term success.

Skill Requirements: Successfully implementing and managing AI-driven automation requires specialized skills and expertise. Recruiting and retaining qualified personnel can be a challenge, particularly in a competitive job market.

6. Ethical and Regulatory Considerations

Ethical Use: Ensuring that AI-driven automation is used ethically involves addressing concerns related to privacy, fairness, and accountability. Developing and adhering to ethical guidelines is crucial for responsible AI use.

Regulatory Compliance: AI-driven automation must comply with relevant regulations and standards. Navigating the regulatory landscape and ensuring that AI systems meet legal requirements is a significant challenge.

Accountability: Establishing clear lines of accountability for AI-driven decisions and actions is important for addressing potential issues and ensuring that systems are used responsibly.

7. Best Practices for Addressing Challenges

Data Governance: Implement robust data governance practices to ensure data quality, integrity, and security. Establish processes for data collection, management, and protection.

Bias Mitigation: Develop and implement strategies to detect and mitigate bias in AI systems. Regularly evaluate algorithms and data for fairness and equity.

Integration Planning: Carefully plan and manage the integration of AI-driven automation with existing systems. Ensure that infrastructure and compatibility issues are addressed before implementation.

Explainability and Transparency: Invest in methods for explainable AI and provide clear communication about how AI systems make decisions. Build trust through transparency and accountability.

Cost Management: Evaluate the cost-benefit ratio of AI-driven automation and plan for both initial investments and ongoing maintenance. Consider scalability and long-term financial implications.

Ethical and Regulatory Compliance: Develop and adhere to ethical guidelines and ensure compliance with regulatory requirements. Stay informed about evolving regulations and industry standards.

Skill Development: Invest in training and development for staff to build the necessary skills and expertise for managing and utilizing AI-driven automation effectively.

Implementing AI-driven automation presents several challenges, including data quality, algorithmic bias, system integration, interpretability, cost, and ethical considerations. Addressing these challenges requires careful planning, robust governance, and ongoing evaluation. By adopting best practices and ensuring that AI systems are implemented responsibly and transparently, organizations can overcome these challenges and harness the full potential of AI-driven automation to enhance efficiency, accuracy, and scalability in their operations.

Chapter 7: Ethical Considerations in AI and OSINT

Chapter 7, "Ethical Considerations in AI and OSINT," examines the crucial ethical issues that arise with the integration of Artificial Intelligence (AI) into Open Source Intelligence (OSINT) practices. This chapter addresses concerns such as privacy, data protection, and algorithmic bias, emphasizing the need for responsible use of AI technologies in cyber investigations. It explores how ethical considerations impact decision-making and the implementation of AI-driven tools, advocating for transparency, accountability, and fairness in their application. By highlighting the balance between leveraging AI for enhanced intelligence and maintaining ethical standards, the chapter provides a framework for navigating the complex moral landscape of modern cyber investigations.

7.1. Ethical Issues in AI-Enhanced OSINT

Open Source Intelligence (OSINT), when enhanced by Artificial Intelligence (AI), offers powerful tools for gathering, analyzing, and interpreting publicly available information. However, the integration of AI into OSINT raises several ethical concerns that need to be carefully considered and addressed. This section explores the key ethical issues associated with AI-enhanced OSINT, highlighting the complexities and implications for privacy, fairness, accountability, and transparency.

1. Privacy Concerns

Data Collection and Surveillance: AI-enhanced OSINT tools can collect and analyze vast amounts of data from public sources, including social media, websites, and online forums. While this data is publicly accessible, its extensive collection and analysis can raise privacy concerns, particularly if individuals are unaware of how their data is being used.

Personal Information: AI tools can aggregate and analyze personal information, such as social media profiles and online activities, potentially revealing sensitive details about individuals. The ethical challenge is to balance the need for information with respect for individuals' privacy.

Consent and Awareness: Individuals may not be aware that their data is being collected and analyzed by AI-driven OSINT tools. Ethical use of AI in OSINT should involve transparent practices and respect for individuals' rights to control their own information.

2. Bias and Fairness

Algorithmic Bias: AI systems can inherit biases present in the data they are trained on. This can lead to biased analyses and decisions that disproportionately affect certain groups or individuals. For example, biased data could result in unfair targeting or profiling.

Fairness in Analysis: Ensuring fairness in AI-driven OSINT requires addressing potential biases in data sources and algorithms. This involves developing and implementing strategies to detect and mitigate bias, as well as ensuring that AI systems are used equitably.

Impact on Marginalized Groups: AI-enhanced OSINT can disproportionately impact marginalized or vulnerable groups. Ethical considerations should include assessing and mitigating the potential negative effects of AI analyses on these groups.

3. Accountability and Transparency

Decision-Making Responsibility: Determining who is responsible for decisions made based on AI-enhanced OSINT is crucial. Accountability issues arise when AI systems make recommendations or decisions that affect individuals or organizations.

Transparency of Algorithms: The "black box" nature of some AI algorithms can make it difficult to understand how decisions are made. Ensuring transparency in AI-driven OSINT involves providing clear explanations of how algorithms work and how decisions are reached.

Auditing and Oversight: Implementing mechanisms for auditing and oversight of AI-enhanced OSINT processes helps ensure that ethical standards are upheld. Regular reviews and assessments can identify and address potential issues related to accountability and transparency.

4. Misuse and Malpractice

Potential for Abuse: AI-enhanced OSINT tools have the potential for misuse, such as for surveillance, stalking, or harassment. Ethical use involves establishing safeguards to prevent abuse and ensure that AI tools are used for legitimate purposes.

Weaponization of OSINT: AI-enhanced OSINT could be weaponized for malicious activities, such as targeting political opponents or manipulating public opinion. Ethical considerations include preventing the weaponization of OSINT and ensuring that AI tools are used responsibly.

Accuracy and Reliability: Ensuring the accuracy and reliability of AI-enhanced OSINT is essential to avoid misinformation and false conclusions. Ethical use requires implementing measures to verify and validate the information generated by AI systems.

5. Legal and Regulatory Compliance

Adherence to Regulations: AI-enhanced OSINT must comply with legal and regulatory requirements related to data protection, privacy, and surveillance. Ethical use involves staying informed about relevant laws and ensuring that AI practices adhere to legal standards.

Ethical Guidelines and Standards: Developing and following ethical guidelines and standards for AI-enhanced OSINT helps ensure that practices are aligned with societal values and expectations. This includes addressing ethical concerns related to data collection, analysis, and use.

Cross-Border Issues: AI-enhanced OSINT may involve data from multiple jurisdictions, raising complex legal and ethical issues. Ensuring compliance with international regulations and respecting diverse legal frameworks is crucial.

6. Best Practices for Ethical AI-Enhanced OSINT

Establish Clear Policies and Procedures: Develop and implement policies and procedures for ethical AI-enhanced OSINT, including guidelines for data collection, analysis, and use. Ensure that these policies address privacy, fairness, and accountability.

Implement Bias Mitigation Strategies: Regularly assess and address biases in AI algorithms and data sources. Implement strategies for detecting and mitigating bias to ensure fair and equitable outcomes.

Ensure Transparency and Explainability: Provide clear explanations of AI algorithms and decision-making processes. Ensure that stakeholders understand how AI-driven OSINT works and how decisions are made.

Maintain Privacy and Consent: Respect individuals' privacy and obtain consent where necessary. Implement measures to protect personal information and ensure that data collection and analysis are conducted responsibly.

Monitor and Review Practices: Continuously monitor and review AI-enhanced OSINT practices to identify and address potential ethical issues. Conduct regular audits and assessments to ensure compliance with ethical standards.

Promote Ethical Training and Awareness: Provide training and resources to stakeholders involved in AI-enhanced OSINT to raise awareness of ethical issues and promote responsible practices.

The integration of AI into OSINT presents significant ethical challenges, including privacy concerns, algorithmic bias, accountability, misuse, and legal compliance. Addressing these challenges requires a commitment to ethical principles and the implementation of best practices. By establishing clear policies, ensuring transparency, and respecting privacy, organizations can leverage the benefits of AI-enhanced OSINT while upholding ethical standards and promoting responsible use.

7.2. Privacy Concerns in AI-Driven Investigations

AI-driven investigations harness advanced technologies to analyze and interpret vast amounts of data, enhancing the speed and accuracy of investigative processes. However, this power raises significant privacy concerns that must be addressed to ensure responsible and ethical use. This section explores the key privacy issues associated with AI-driven investigations, examining their implications and suggesting strategies for mitigating privacy risks.

1. Data Collection and Scope

Broad Data Gathering: AI-driven investigations often involve collecting data from a wide array of sources, including social media, public records, and online interactions. The broad scope of data collection can encompass extensive personal information, raising concerns about the extent to which individuals' data is gathered and analyzed.

Invasive Data Practices: Some AI tools can access and analyze highly personal data, such as communication content or behavioral patterns. This can lead to invasive practices where individuals' private lives are scrutinized without their explicit consent.

Potential for Overreach: The capacity of AI to aggregate and analyze data can lead to overreach, where the amount of data collected exceeds what is necessary for the investigation. Ensuring that data collection is proportionate and relevant is crucial to addressing privacy concerns.

2. Data Privacy and Security

Data Protection: AI-driven investigations must handle sensitive information with stringent data protection measures. Ensuring that data is securely stored, transmitted, and accessed is essential to prevent unauthorized access or breaches.

Risk of Data Breaches: The more data collected and stored, the higher the risk of data breaches. AI systems must implement robust security protocols to safeguard against hacking, data leaks, and other security threats.

Data Retention and Disposal: Proper data retention and disposal practices are crucial to managing privacy risks. Investigations should define clear policies for how long data is retained and ensure secure disposal of data that is no longer needed.

3. Consent and Transparency

Lack of Consent: Individuals often do not provide explicit consent for their data to be collected and analyzed by AI systems in investigations. Ensuring that consent is obtained or that individuals are informed about the use of their data is important for respecting privacy rights.

Transparency of Data Use: Transparency about how data is collected, used, and analyzed by AI systems helps build trust and ensures that individuals understand the scope of data processing. Providing clear information about data practices can address concerns about privacy and accountability.

Notification and Awareness: Informing individuals about their data being used in investigations and providing them with options to opt-out or control the use of their data enhances privacy protection.

4. Data Minimization and Purpose Limitation

Data Minimization: Adopting principles of data minimization involves collecting only the data necessary for the investigation. This reduces the risk of unnecessary exposure of personal information and aligns with privacy best practices.

Purpose Limitation: Data collected for investigative purposes should only be used for those purposes and not for unrelated activities. Ensuring that data is used strictly within the context of the investigation helps protect privacy and prevent misuse.

Anonymization and De-Identification: Anonymizing or de-identifying data where possible can protect individuals' identities while still allowing for meaningful analysis. Implementing these techniques can reduce privacy risks associated with data processing.

5. Ethical and Legal Compliance

Adherence to Privacy Laws: AI-driven investigations must comply with privacy laws and regulations, such as the General Data Protection Regulation (GDPR) or the California Consumer Privacy Act (CCPA). Understanding and adhering to these regulations is crucial for protecting privacy.

Ethical Guidelines: Developing and following ethical guidelines for data collection and analysis helps ensure that AI-driven investigations respect privacy and uphold ethical standards. Guidelines should address consent, transparency, and data protection.

Regulatory Oversight: Regulatory bodies and oversight mechanisms can help ensure that AI-driven investigations are conducted in compliance with privacy laws and ethical standards. Engaging with regulators and adhering to their guidance is important for maintaining privacy and accountability.

6. Best Practices for Addressing Privacy Concerns

Develop Privacy Policies: Establish comprehensive privacy policies that outline how data is collected, used, and protected in AI-driven investigations. Ensure that these policies address consent, data security, and data retention.

Implement Data Protection Measures: Adopt robust data protection measures, including encryption, access controls, and secure storage practices. Regularly review and update security protocols to address emerging threats.

Obtain Consent and Inform Individuals: Where feasible, obtain explicit consent from individuals for data collection and use. Provide clear information about data practices and allow individuals to exercise their privacy rights.

Adopt Data Minimization and Purpose Limitation: Collect only the data necessary for the investigation and use it solely for the intended purposes. Implement data minimization and purpose limitation practices to reduce privacy risks.

Regularly Review and Audit Practices: Conduct regular reviews and audits of AI-driven investigation practices to ensure compliance with privacy policies and regulations. Identify and address potential privacy issues and improve practices as needed.

Promote Transparency and Accountability: Foster transparency by providing information about how AI systems operate and how data is used. Establish accountability mechanisms to address privacy concerns and ensure responsible use of data.

Privacy concerns are a critical aspect of AI-driven investigations, encompassing issues related to data collection, protection, consent, and compliance with legal and ethical standards. Addressing these concerns requires a commitment to privacy best practices, including data minimization, robust security measures, and transparency. By implementing effective privacy policies and practices, organizations can leverage AI-driven investigations while respecting individuals' privacy rights and upholding ethical standards.

7.3. Mitigating Bias in AI Algorithms

Bias in AI algorithms is a significant concern in the development and deployment of artificial intelligence systems. When AI algorithms are biased, they can lead to unfair outcomes, reinforce existing inequalities, and undermine trust in technology. Addressing and mitigating bias is essential to ensure that AI systems are equitable, transparent, and reliable. This section explores the sources of bias in AI algorithms, strategies for mitigation, and best practices for promoting fairness in AI systems.

1. Understanding Sources of Bias

Data Bias: Bias often originates from the data used to train AI models. If the training data reflects existing prejudices or imbalances, the AI system can replicate and perpetuate these biases. For example, biased data can result in discriminatory outcomes in hiring algorithms or facial recognition systems.

Algorithmic Bias: Bias can also arise from the algorithms themselves. The design and implementation of algorithms can introduce biases, particularly if the algorithms are not adequately tested for fairness or if they rely on biased features.

Human Bias: Human decisions during the design, development, and deployment phases can introduce biases. Choices about which data to collect, which features to include, and how to evaluate model performance can all contribute to biased outcomes.

Feedback Loops: AI systems that interact with users can create feedback loops, where biased decisions lead to biased data, further reinforcing the initial biases. For example, biased content recommendations on social media can lead to more exposure to similar biased content.

2. Strategies for Mitigating Bias

Diverse and Representative Data: Ensuring that training data is diverse and representative of different groups and scenarios is crucial for reducing bias. This involves collecting data from a variety of sources and ensuring that all relevant groups are adequately represented.

Bias Detection and Testing: Implementing techniques for detecting and testing bias in AI algorithms is essential. This includes using fairness metrics and auditing tools to evaluate whether AI systems produce equitable outcomes across different demographic groups.

Algorithmic Fairness Techniques: Applying algorithmic fairness techniques, such as reweighting training data, adjusting decision thresholds, or using fairness constraints, can help address biases. These techniques aim to balance the impact of AI decisions across different groups.

Bias Mitigation Frameworks: Utilizing established frameworks and guidelines for bias mitigation, such as the Fairness, Accountability, and Transparency (FAT) principles, can provide structured approaches to addressing bias. These frameworks offer best practices and methodologies for developing fair AI systems.

Human Oversight and Review: Incorporating human oversight and review into the AI development process can help identify and address biases. Involving diverse teams in the design and evaluation phases can provide different perspectives and reduce the risk of biased outcomes.

Transparent Reporting and Documentation: Maintaining transparency about the data, algorithms, and processes used in AI systems is important for accountability. Providing clear documentation and reporting on bias mitigation efforts helps stakeholders understand how biases are addressed and managed.

3. Best Practices for Promoting Fairness

Implement Fairness Audits: Conduct regular fairness audits of AI systems to assess their performance and identify potential biases. Audits should include evaluating the impact of AI decisions on different demographic groups and addressing any disparities found.

Engage Stakeholders: Engage stakeholders, including affected communities and subject matter experts, in the development and evaluation of AI systems. This collaboration can provide valuable insights into potential biases and help ensure that AI systems meet fairness standards.

Educate and Train Teams: Provide training and education for AI developers and data scientists on bias and fairness. This includes raising awareness about the sources of bias, bias mitigation techniques, and the ethical implications of biased AI systems.

Develop Inclusive Policies: Create and enforce policies that promote fairness and inclusivity in AI development. These policies should address bias detection, mitigation, and reporting and ensure that all team members adhere to ethical standards.

Monitor and Adapt: Continuously monitor AI systems for emerging biases and adapt mitigation strategies as needed. Bias mitigation is an ongoing process that requires regular review and adjustment to address new challenges and changing contexts.

Promote Ethical AI Practices: Foster a culture of ethical AI development by prioritizing fairness, accountability, and transparency. Encourage the adoption of ethical principles and best practices throughout the AI lifecycle.

4. Case Studies and Real-World Examples

Bias in Facial Recognition: Studies have shown that facial recognition systems can exhibit significant biases, such as higher error rates for individuals with darker skin tones. Addressing this issue involves improving training data diversity, implementing fairness techniques, and conducting thorough bias evaluations.

Gender Bias in Hiring Algorithms: Some hiring algorithms have been found to favor male candidates over female candidates due to biased training data. Mitigation strategies include using gender-neutral data, applying fairness constraints, and regularly auditing algorithmic outcomes.

Racial Bias in Predictive Policing: Predictive policing systems have been criticized for perpetuating racial biases present in historical crime data. Mitigating these biases involves refining data sources, applying fairness techniques, and ensuring transparency in decision-making processes.

Mitigating bias in AI algorithms is essential for developing fair, transparent, and accountable AI systems. By understanding the sources of bias, implementing effective mitigation strategies, and following best practices for fairness, organizations can reduce the risk of biased outcomes and promote equity in AI-driven decision-making. Addressing bias is an ongoing process that requires continuous monitoring, stakeholder engagement, and a commitment to ethical AI practices. Through these efforts, AI systems can better serve all individuals and communities, fostering trust and ensuring that technology benefits everyone equitably.

7.4. Ensuring Transparency in AI Applications

Transparency in AI applications is crucial for fostering trust, accountability, and ethical use of technology. It involves making the workings, decisions, and impacts of AI systems clear and understandable to users, stakeholders, and the public. Ensuring transparency helps to mitigate risks, prevent misuse, and enhance the credibility of AI systems. This section explores the key aspects of transparency in AI applications, including the principles, challenges, and best practices for promoting openness and clarity.

1. Principles of Transparency

Clarity of Purpose: AI systems should have a clearly defined purpose, and this purpose should be communicated transparently. Users and stakeholders should understand why the AI system exists, what problems it aims to solve, and how it is expected to perform.

Explainability of Algorithms: Transparency requires that AI algorithms be explainable, meaning that their decision-making processes can be understood and interpreted. Explainability involves providing insights into how algorithms generate their outputs, including the factors and data that influence decisions.

Disclosure of Data Sources: Transparency involves disclosing the sources of data used to train and evaluate AI models. Users should be informed about where data comes from, how it was collected, and any potential limitations or biases associated with the data.

Visibility of Model Training and Evaluation: Information about how AI models are trained and evaluated should be accessible. This includes details about the training data, model architecture, performance metrics, and validation processes.

Accessibility of Documentation: Comprehensive documentation of AI systems should be made available to stakeholders. This documentation should include explanations of the system's design, functionality, and limitations, as well as any relevant ethical considerations.

2. Challenges to Transparency

Complexity of AI Systems: AI systems, especially those based on deep learning, can be highly complex and operate as "black boxes," making it difficult to understand and explain their inner workings. The complexity of algorithms and models poses a challenge to achieving transparency.

Proprietary Information: Some organizations may be reluctant to disclose detailed information about their AI systems due to concerns about protecting intellectual property or competitive advantage. Balancing transparency with the protection of proprietary information can be challenging.

Technical Limitations: The current state of AI research and technology may limit the extent to which certain algorithms can be explained or understood. Developing techniques for explainable AI (XAI) is an ongoing area of research aimed at addressing these limitations.

Regulatory and Legal Constraints: Different jurisdictions may have varying requirements for transparency in AI applications. Navigating legal and regulatory constraints while maintaining transparency can be complex, especially for global organizations.

User Understanding: Even when AI systems are transparent, users may struggle to understand complex explanations or technical details. Ensuring that explanations are accessible and comprehensible to non-expert users is an important aspect of transparency.

3. Best Practices for Promoting Transparency

Adopt Explainable AI (XAI) Techniques: Implement explainable AI techniques that provide insights into how models make decisions. Techniques such as feature importance analysis, decision trees, and model interpretability tools can help make AI systems more transparent.

Provide Clear and Accessible Documentation: Develop and maintain clear, accessible documentation that explains the purpose, design, and functionality of AI systems. Ensure that documentation is written in plain language and is easily accessible to users and stakeholders.

Disclose Data Sources and Limitations: Clearly disclose the sources of data used in AI systems, including any limitations or biases associated with the data. Provide information about data collection methods, data quality, and any potential impact on system performance.

Implement Transparency Reports: Publish transparency reports that provide an overview of AI system operations, performance, and impact. These reports can include information about model accuracy, fairness, and any incidents or issues encountered.

Engage with Stakeholders: Engage with stakeholders, including users, affected communities, and regulatory bodies, to gather feedback and address transparency concerns. Involving stakeholders in the development and evaluation of AI systems can help ensure that transparency needs are met.

Develop User-Friendly Explanations: Create user-friendly explanations of AI system decisions and actions. Use visualizations, simplified language, and interactive tools to help users understand how AI systems work and how decisions are made.

Ensure Compliance with Regulations: Stay informed about legal and regulatory requirements related to transparency in AI applications. Ensure that AI systems comply with relevant regulations and standards, and adapt transparency practices as needed.

4. Case Studies and Real-World Examples

IBM's AI Explainability 360 Toolkit: IBM developed the AI Explainability 360 Toolkit, which provides a set of tools and techniques for enhancing the explainability of AI models. This toolkit helps organizations understand and communicate how their AI systems make decisions.

Google's Model Cards: Google introduced Model Cards, a form of documentation that provides information about AI models, including their intended use, performance, and limitations. Model Cards aim to improve transparency and help users make informed decisions about AI systems.

Microsoft's Fairness Checklist: Microsoft created the Fairness Checklist, which outlines best practices for ensuring fairness and transparency in AI systems. The checklist provides guidelines for documenting data sources, evaluating model performance, and addressing potential biases.

Ensuring transparency in AI applications is essential for building trust, accountability, and ethical use of technology. By adopting explainable AI techniques, providing clear documentation, disclosing data sources, and engaging with stakeholders, organizations can enhance the transparency of their AI systems. Addressing challenges related to complexity, proprietary information, and user understanding requires ongoing effort and commitment. Through these practices, AI systems can become more transparent, understandable, and aligned with ethical standards, ultimately benefiting users and promoting responsible AI development.

7.5. The Importance of Accountability in AI Use

Accountability in AI use is crucial for ensuring that artificial intelligence systems are developed, deployed, and managed in a responsible and ethical manner. It involves taking responsibility for the decisions and actions of AI systems, addressing potential negative impacts, and ensuring that AI technologies are used in ways that align with legal, ethical, and societal norms. This section explores the importance of accountability in AI use, the key aspects of accountability, and best practices for fostering responsible AI practices.

1. Understanding Accountability in AI

Definition and Scope: Accountability in AI refers to the obligation of individuals, organizations, and entities to take responsibility for the outcomes and impacts of AI systems. It encompasses ensuring that AI technologies are used ethically, transparently, and in compliance with laws and regulations.

Responsibility for Decisions: AI systems can make decisions that affect individuals and society, such as in hiring, lending, or law enforcement. Accountability involves ensuring that those who design, implement, and use AI systems are answerable for the consequences of these decisions.

Addressing Harm and Redress: Accountability includes addressing any harm caused by AI systems and providing mechanisms for redress. This means having processes in place to correct mistakes, mitigate negative impacts, and offer remedies to affected parties.

2. Key Aspects of Accountability

Clear Ownership and Governance: Establishing clear ownership and governance structures for AI projects is fundamental to accountability. This involves defining roles and responsibilities for those involved in the development, deployment, and oversight of AI systems.

Transparency and Documentation: Maintaining transparency about how AI systems are developed and used is a key aspect of accountability. This includes documenting the design, data sources, algorithms, and decision-making processes of AI systems.

Ethical Standards and Compliance: Ensuring that AI systems adhere to ethical standards and comply with legal and regulatory requirements is critical for accountability. This involves integrating ethical considerations into AI development and operations and ensuring compliance with relevant laws and regulations.

Impact Assessment and Monitoring: Regularly assessing and monitoring the impact of AI systems helps to identify and address potential issues. Impact assessments should evaluate the social, ethical, and legal implications of AI systems and ensure that they are functioning as intended.

Feedback Mechanisms and Redress: Implementing mechanisms for feedback and redress allows stakeholders to report issues, provide input, and seek remedies. This includes creating channels for users to voice concerns and having processes in place to address complaints and rectify problems.

3. Best Practices for Ensuring Accountability

Develop Accountability Frameworks: Create frameworks that outline the principles and practices for ensuring accountability in AI use. These frameworks should define roles, responsibilities, and procedures for managing AI systems and addressing any issues that arise.

Implement Robust Governance Structures: Establish governance structures that provide oversight and accountability for AI projects. This includes appointing dedicated teams or individuals responsible for managing AI systems and ensuring that they adhere to ethical and legal standards.

Conduct Regular Audits and Reviews: Perform regular audits and reviews of AI systems to assess their performance, compliance, and impact. Audits should evaluate whether AI systems are operating as intended and identify any areas for improvement or correction.

Promote Ethical AI Development: Integrate ethical considerations into the development and deployment of AI systems. This includes adhering to ethical guidelines, conducting impact assessments, and ensuring that AI systems are designed and used in ways that respect human rights and societal values.

Ensure Transparency in Decision-Making: Provide clear and accessible information about how AI systems make decisions and the factors that influence these decisions. Transparency helps stakeholders understand and trust AI systems and enables them to hold developers and users accountable.

Facilitate Stakeholder Engagement: Engage with stakeholders, including users, affected communities, and regulatory bodies, to gather feedback and address accountability concerns. Involving stakeholders in the development and evaluation of AI systems helps ensure that their perspectives are considered and that accountability mechanisms are effective.

Establish Redress Mechanisms: Create mechanisms for addressing grievances and providing remedies for harm caused by AI systems. This includes setting up processes for users to report issues, seek compensation, and receive support in case of adverse outcomes.

Train and Educate AI Professionals: Provide training and education for AI professionals on accountability, ethical standards, and best practices. Ensuring that those involved in AI development and deployment understand their responsibilities and obligations is essential for fostering accountability.

4. Case Studies and Real-World Examples

Autonomous Vehicles and Liability: The deployment of autonomous vehicles has raised questions about liability and accountability in case of accidents. Establishing clear frameworks for determining responsibility and ensuring that manufacturers and operators are accountable for vehicle performance and safety is crucial.

AI in Hiring and Recruitment: AI systems used in hiring and recruitment can perpetuate biases and discrimination. Implementing accountability measures, such as bias audits and transparency reports, helps ensure that these systems are fair and do not result in unfair treatment of candidates.

Facial Recognition Technology: The use of facial recognition technology has sparked debates about privacy and accountability. Addressing these concerns involves implementing transparency about data use, ensuring compliance with privacy laws, and providing mechanisms for individuals to challenge and seek redress for wrongful uses of the technology.

Ensuring accountability in AI use is essential for fostering responsible and ethical AI practices. By establishing clear ownership and governance structures, maintaining transparency, adhering to ethical standards, and implementing robust feedback and redress mechanisms, organizations can uphold accountability and address potential issues effectively. Accountability involves taking responsibility for the impacts of AI systems, ensuring compliance with laws and regulations, and addressing any harm caused. Through these practices, AI technologies can be developed and used in ways that are fair, transparent, and aligned with societal values, ultimately building trust and confidence in AI systems.

Chapter 8: Legal and Regulatory Frameworks

Chapter 8, "Legal and Regulatory Frameworks," explores the complex legal and regulatory landscape surrounding the use of Artificial Intelligence (AI) in Open Source Intelligence (OSINT). This chapter provides an overview of global regulations and compliance issues relevant to AI-driven cyber investigations, including data protection laws, privacy requirements, and legal constraints. It discusses how various jurisdictions approach the use of AI in intelligence gathering and the implications for practitioners. By understanding these legal frameworks, readers can navigate the challenges of integrating AI into OSINT while ensuring adherence to legal standards and safeguarding ethical practices.

8.1. Legal Implications of AI in OSINT

The integration of artificial intelligence (AI) in Open Source Intelligence (OSINT) brings significant advantages in data collection, analysis, and decision-making. However, it also introduces complex legal challenges that must be carefully navigated to ensure compliance with existing laws and regulations. This section explores the key legal implications of using AI in OSINT, focusing on privacy, data protection, intellectual property, and the evolving legal landscape.

1. Privacy Concerns and Data Protection

Personal Data Collection: OSINT often involves the collection and analysis of publicly available information, which can include personal data. When AI is used to enhance these processes, the scale and scope of data collection increase dramatically, raising concerns about privacy. The use of AI in OSINT must comply with data protection laws such as the General Data Protection Regulation (GDPR) in Europe, which imposes strict rules on the collection, processing, and storage of personal data.

Surveillance and Intrusion: AI-powered OSINT tools can inadvertently cross the line into surveillance, especially when they aggregate data from multiple sources to create detailed profiles of individuals. This raises legal and ethical questions about the balance between intelligence gathering and the right to privacy. Ensuring that AI-driven OSINT activities do not constitute unlawful surveillance is essential to avoid legal repercussions.

Data Minimization and Purpose Limitation: Legal frameworks often emphasize the principles of data minimization and purpose limitation, requiring that only the minimum amount of data necessary for a specific purpose is collected and used. AI systems in OSINT must be designed to adhere to these principles, ensuring that data collection and processing are proportionate and justified by the intended use.

2. Intellectual Property and Data Ownership

Use of Proprietary Data: AI in OSINT may involve analyzing data that is subject to intellectual property rights, such as copyrighted content or proprietary databases. Legal implications arise when AI systems scrape, process, or use such data without proper authorization or licensing. Organizations must be aware of the intellectual property rights associated with the data they use and ensure that their AI systems operate within the bounds of the law.

Creation of Derivative Works: AI systems in OSINT can generate new insights, reports, or content based on the analysis of existing data. The legal status of these outputs, particularly whether they constitute derivative works subject to copyright protection, can be complex. Organizations must consider the intellectual property implications of AI-generated content and ensure that they respect the rights of original content creators.

Data Ownership and Sharing: Questions of data ownership become more complicated when AI processes data from multiple sources. Determining who owns the data, the insights generated, and the AI models themselves is crucial for compliance with legal and contractual obligations. Organizations using AI in OSINT must establish clear data ownership and sharing agreements to avoid disputes and legal challenges.

3. Compliance with Regulatory Frameworks

Adherence to National and International Laws: The use of AI in OSINT must comply with a complex web of national and international laws that govern data privacy, cybersecurity, and intelligence activities. Organizations must be aware of the legal requirements in the jurisdictions where they operate and ensure that their AI systems adhere to applicable laws. This includes not only data protection laws but also laws related to national security, export controls, and anti-terrorism measures.

Regulation of AI and Automated Decision-Making: As AI technology evolves, regulatory bodies are increasingly focusing on the governance of AI and automated decision-making systems. Regulations such as the European Union's proposed AI Act aim to ensure that AI systems are transparent, accountable, and free from bias. Organizations using AI in OSINT must stay informed about emerging regulations and be prepared to adapt their practices to remain compliant.

Cross-Border Data Transfers: AI in OSINT often involves the transfer of data across borders, which can trigger legal issues related to data sovereignty and jurisdiction. Regulations such as the GDPR impose strict rules on the transfer of personal data to countries outside the European Economic Area (EEA). Organizations must ensure that their AI systems and data transfer practices comply with relevant cross-border data transfer laws to avoid penalties and legal disputes.

4. Ethical and Legal Accountability

Bias and Discrimination: AI systems in OSINT can inadvertently perpetuate or exacerbate biases present in the data they analyze. This can lead to discriminatory outcomes, raising both ethical and legal concerns. Organizations must take steps to mitigate bias in their AI systems, including implementing fairness checks and ensuring that their algorithms do not result in unlawful discrimination.

Transparency and Explainability: Legal frameworks increasingly emphasize the need for transparency and explainability in AI systems. Organizations must be able to explain how their AI systems make decisions, particularly when those decisions have significant legal or ethical implications. Ensuring that AI systems in OSINT are transparent and explainable is crucial for legal compliance and maintaining public trust.

Accountability for AI Decisions: As AI systems become more autonomous, questions of accountability become more complex. Determining who is responsible for the decisions made by AI systems in OSINT is a key legal challenge. Organizations must establish clear accountability frameworks that outline the responsibilities of developers, users, and other stakeholders involved in the deployment of AI in OSINT.

5. The Evolving Legal Landscape

Legislative Developments: The legal landscape surrounding AI and OSINT is rapidly evolving, with new laws and regulations being proposed and enacted worldwide. Organizations must stay informed about these developments and be prepared to adapt their practices accordingly. This includes monitoring legislative initiatives related to AI, data protection, cybersecurity, and intelligence activities.

Judicial Interpretations: Court decisions play a crucial role in shaping the legal framework for AI and OSINT. Judicial interpretations of existing laws can provide clarity on how legal principles apply to AI technologies, but they can also introduce new legal uncertainties. Organizations must keep track of relevant case law and be prepared to respond to legal challenges.

International Cooperation and Harmonization: The global nature of AI and OSINT activities requires international cooperation and the harmonization of legal standards. Organizations operating across borders must navigate varying legal requirements and seek to comply with international agreements and guidelines. Engaging in dialogue with regulators and participating in industry efforts to harmonize legal standards can help organizations manage the legal implications of AI in OSINT.

The use of AI in OSINT offers significant benefits for cyber investigations and intelligence gathering, but it also raises complex legal challenges. Privacy concerns, data protection, intellectual property rights, regulatory compliance, and ethical accountability are all critical considerations for organizations leveraging AI in OSINT. As the legal landscape continues to evolve, organizations must remain vigilant and proactive in addressing these challenges to ensure that their AI-driven OSINT practices are legally compliant, ethically sound, and socially responsible. By navigating the legal implications effectively, organizations can harness the power of AI in OSINT while upholding the principles of justice, fairness, and accountability.

8.2. Global Regulations on AI and Cyber Investigations

As artificial intelligence (AI) continues to advance and its applications in cyber investigations become more widespread, regulatory frameworks across the globe are evolving to address the unique challenges and risks associated with these technologies. The global landscape of AI regulations is characterized by a diverse set of laws, guidelines, and standards, each aimed at ensuring the ethical and responsible use of AI while protecting privacy, security, and human rights. This section explores the key global regulations on AI and cyber investigations, focusing on prominent regional and international efforts to govern AI's role in cybersecurity.

1. European Union: Leading the Way in AI Regulation

The General Data Protection Regulation (GDPR): The GDPR is one of the most comprehensive data protection laws in the world, with significant implications for AI in cyber investigations. It imposes strict rules on data processing, including the use of AI for automated decision-making. Under the GDPR, organizations must ensure that AI systems used in cyber investigations respect individual privacy rights, provide transparency, and offer mechanisms for individuals to challenge or appeal automated decisions.

The AI Act: The European Union's proposed AI Act is a pioneering piece of legislation that seeks to regulate AI technologies based on their potential risks. The AI Act categorizes AI systems into four risk levels—unacceptable, high, limited, and minimal—and imposes varying degrees of regulatory requirements. For AI used in cyber investigations, particularly in law enforcement or national security contexts, the AI Act is likely to impose stringent oversight, transparency, and accountability measures to prevent abuse and ensure compliance with fundamental rights.

The Network and Information Security (NIS2) Directive: The NIS2 Directive is focused on strengthening cybersecurity across the EU. It sets standards for network and information security, which include requirements for AI-driven systems used in cyber investigations. Organizations using AI in cybersecurity must comply with the NIS2 Directive's guidelines on securing data, protecting critical infrastructure, and responding to cyber threats.

2. United States: Sector-Specific and State-Level Approaches

The Algorithmic Accountability Act: Proposed in the United States, the Algorithmic Accountability Act would require companies to conduct impact assessments on AI systems, particularly those used in sensitive areas such as cybersecurity. The goal is to identify and mitigate biases, ensure transparency, and protect consumer rights. Although this act has not yet been passed into law, it reflects a growing interest in regulating AI at the federal level.

State-Level Initiatives: Various U.S. states, including California and New York, have introduced their own AI-related regulations. For example, California's Consumer Privacy Act (CCPA) includes provisions that affect how AI systems handle personal data in cyber investigations. Additionally, New York City has enacted legislation requiring companies to disclose the use of AI in employment decisions, which could extend to AI tools used in internal cybersecurity investigations.

Sectoral Regulations: The U.S. approach to AI regulation is often sector-specific. For example, the Health Insurance Portability and Accountability Act (HIPAA) governs the use of AI in healthcare cybersecurity, while the Gramm-Leach-Bliley Act (GLBA) applies to financial institutions. These regulations require that AI systems used in cyber investigations within these sectors adhere to strict data security and privacy standards.

3. Asia: Emerging Frameworks and Guidelines

China's AI Guidelines: China has rapidly developed AI technologies and is now focusing on creating regulatory frameworks to manage their use. The country's approach to AI regulation is heavily influenced by its broader policies on cybersecurity and national security. China's guidelines emphasize state control over AI technologies, particularly in areas like cyber investigations and law enforcement. Organizations operating in China must comply with stringent government oversight and data localization requirements.

Singapore's AI Governance Framework: Singapore has positioned itself as a leader in AI governance in Asia, with a framework that promotes the ethical use of AI while encouraging innovation. The framework outlines key principles for AI use, including transparency, fairness, and accountability. In the context of cyber investigations, Singapore's approach emphasizes the importance of protecting personal data and ensuring that AI systems do not infringe on individual rights.

Japan's AI Strategy: Japan has developed a national AI strategy that includes guidelines for the ethical use of AI in various sectors, including cybersecurity. The strategy highlights the need for AI systems to be transparent, accountable, and secure. Japan's regulatory approach is also informed by its commitment to international cooperation, with a focus on harmonizing AI standards with those of other countries.

4. International Efforts: Harmonizing AI Regulations

The Organisation for Economic Co-operation and Development (OECD) Principles on AI: The OECD has established a set of principles to guide the development and use of AI technologies globally. These principles emphasize the need for AI systems to be inclusive, transparent, and accountable, with a strong focus on respecting human rights. For AI in cyber investigations, the OECD principles provide a framework for ensuring that AI technologies are used responsibly and do not contribute to human rights violations.

The Global Partnership on AI (GPAI): The GPAI is an international initiative that brings together governments, industry, and academia to promote the responsible use of AI. The partnership focuses on developing best practices for AI governance, including in areas like cybersecurity. Through collaborative efforts, the GPAI aims to create a harmonized approach to AI regulation that balances innovation with ethical considerations.

The United Nations (UN) Initiatives: The UN has also taken steps to address the global implications of AI, particularly in the context of security and human rights. The UN has called for a moratorium on certain AI technologies, such as autonomous weapons, until appropriate regulatory frameworks are in place. For cyber investigations, the UN emphasizes the need for AI systems to be governed by international human rights standards and to ensure that they do not exacerbate existing inequalities.

5. Challenges and Opportunities in Global AI Regulation

Divergent Regulatory Approaches: One of the key challenges in global AI regulation is the divergence in approaches between different regions and countries. While the EU is leading with comprehensive legislation like the AI Act, other regions, such as the U.S. and Asia, are taking more sector-specific or state-level approaches. This divergence can create challenges for organizations operating internationally, as they must navigate a complex and often inconsistent regulatory landscape.

Harmonization and International Cooperation: Despite these challenges, there are significant opportunities for harmonization and international cooperation. Efforts like the OECD Principles on AI and the GPAI are paving the way for more consistent global standards. Organizations can benefit from engaging in international dialogue and aligning their AI practices with emerging global norms to ensure compliance and build trust.

Balancing Innovation with Regulation: Another challenge is balancing the need for regulation with the desire to foster innovation. Overly restrictive regulations can stifle the development of AI technologies, while insufficient oversight can lead to misuse and harm. Finding the right balance is crucial for ensuring that AI can be harnessed effectively in cyber investigations without compromising ethical and legal standards.

The global regulatory landscape for AI in cyber investigations is complex and rapidly evolving. From the comprehensive frameworks in the European Union to the sector-specific regulations in the United States and emerging guidelines in Asia, there is a clear recognition of the need to govern AI technologies responsibly. International efforts are also playing a critical role in harmonizing standards and promoting ethical AI use. Organizations must stay informed about these developments and proactively adapt their practices to navigate the legal and regulatory challenges associated with AI in cyber investigations. By doing so, they can leverage AI's full potential while ensuring compliance with global norms and safeguarding the rights and interests of individuals.

8.3. Data Protection Laws and OSINT

Open Source Intelligence (OSINT) involves the collection, analysis, and use of publicly available information to support various intelligence and cybersecurity activities. While OSINT offers significant benefits for cyber investigations, it also presents challenges, particularly in the context of data protection laws. As OSINT operations often involve handling personal data, they must comply with global data protection regulations designed to safeguard individual privacy and data rights. This section explores the intersection of data protection laws and OSINT, examining key legal requirements, challenges, and best practices for ensuring compliance.

1. Overview of Key Data Protection Laws

General Data Protection Regulation (GDPR) - European Union: The GDPR is one of the most comprehensive and influential data protection laws globally, setting strict rules for the processing of personal data within the European Union (EU) and beyond. For OSINT activities, the GDPR requires that any personal data collected, processed, or stored must be done so lawfully, transparently, and with respect for individual rights. This includes obtaining consent when necessary, ensuring data minimization, and providing individuals with rights such as access, rectification, and erasure of their data.

California Consumer Privacy Act (CCPA) - United States: The CCPA provides California residents with specific rights regarding their personal data, including the right to know what data is being collected, the right to delete personal data, and the right to opt-out of the sale of their data. OSINT practitioners operating in California or handling data from California residents must comply with the CCPA's requirements, particularly in terms of transparency and respecting consumer rights.

Personal Information Protection and Electronic Documents Act (PIPEDA) - Canada: PIPEDA governs how private sector organizations in Canada collect, use, and disclose personal information in the course of commercial activities. OSINT activities under PIPEDA must ensure that personal information is collected with consent, used for specified purposes, and protected through appropriate security measures. Additionally, individuals have the right to access their personal information and request corrections if necessary.

Data Protection Act 2018 - United Kingdom: The UK's Data Protection Act 2018 incorporates the principles of the GDPR into UK law, with additional provisions that address specific national issues. OSINT operations in the UK must adhere to these principles, ensuring that personal data is processed fairly, transparently, and securely. The Act also introduces additional obligations, such as those related to law enforcement processing and national security.

Lei Geral de Proteção de Dados (LGPD) - Brazil: Brazil's LGPD is similar to the GDPR and applies to the processing of personal data within Brazil. The LGPD requires that personal data be processed for legitimate purposes, with appropriate safeguards in place. For OSINT practitioners, this means ensuring that any data collected from Brazilian citizens is done so in compliance with the LGPD's provisions, including respecting individuals' rights to access, correct, and delete their data.

2. Legal Requirements for OSINT Under Data Protection Laws

Lawfulness, Fairness, and Transparency: Data protection laws generally require that personal data be processed lawfully, fairly, and transparently. For OSINT, this means that organizations must have a valid legal basis for collecting and processing personal data. Common legal bases include obtaining consent, fulfilling a legal obligation, protecting vital interests, or pursuing legitimate interests. Transparency is also crucial, as individuals must be informed about how their data is being used, especially in cases where data is collected indirectly through OSINT activities.

Data Minimization and Purpose Limitation: Data protection laws emphasize the principles of data minimization and purpose limitation. This means that only the minimum amount of personal data necessary for a specific purpose should be collected, and the data should only be used for that purpose. In OSINT, practitioners must carefully define the scope of their data collection activities and ensure that they do not collect or process more data than is required for the intended investigation or analysis.

Rights of Data Subjects: Individuals have various rights under data protection laws, including the right to access their data, the right to correct inaccuracies, the right to object to processing, and the right to have their data erased (the "right to be forgotten"). OSINT practitioners must implement procedures to respond to these rights in a timely and effective manner. For instance, if an individual requests access to or deletion of their data, the organization must be able to comply with these requests, even if the data was collected through public sources.

Security and Confidentiality: Data protection laws require organizations to implement appropriate technical and organizational measures to ensure the security and confidentiality of personal data. In the context of OSINT, this means that data must be stored securely, access to the data must be controlled, and measures must be in place to prevent unauthorized access, alteration, or loss of data. Additionally, organizations should conduct regular risk assessments and implement data protection impact assessments (DPIAs) for high-risk processing activities.

Cross-Border Data Transfers: Many data protection laws impose restrictions on the transfer of personal data across borders, particularly to countries that do not offer an adequate level of data protection. For OSINT practitioners, this can present challenges, especially when collecting data from global sources. Organizations must ensure that any cross-border data transfers comply with applicable legal requirements, such as using standard contractual clauses, obtaining explicit consent, or relying on adequacy decisions.

3. Challenges of Applying Data Protection Laws to OSINT

Defining Personal Data in OSINT Context: One of the challenges in applying data protection laws to OSINT is defining what constitutes personal data. OSINT often involves the collection of information that may not be directly identifiable but can be combined with other data to identify individuals. This raises questions about when data protection laws apply and how organizations should handle ambiguous cases where the identifiability of data is uncertain.

Balancing Intelligence Needs with Privacy Rights: OSINT is often used in cybersecurity and intelligence contexts, where the need for information may conflict with privacy rights. Organizations must balance these competing interests, ensuring that their OSINT activities are necessary, proportionate, and conducted with respect for individual rights. This is particularly important in law enforcement and national security investigations, where the stakes are high, but so are the potential risks to privacy.

Complying with Multiple Jurisdictions: OSINT practitioners often operate across multiple jurisdictions, each with its own data protection laws. Ensuring compliance with these diverse legal requirements can be complex and resource-intensive. Organizations must develop robust compliance frameworks that account for the specific requirements of each jurisdiction in which they operate, including obtaining legal advice and conducting regular audits to ensure ongoing compliance.

Anonymization and Pseudonymization: Anonymization and pseudonymization are techniques used to protect personal data by removing or masking identifiers. However, in the OSINT context, achieving true anonymization can be difficult, especially when dealing with large datasets that may be re-identified through data aggregation or analysis. Organizations must carefully consider how to apply these techniques in a way that complies with data protection laws while still enabling effective OSINT activities.

Responding to Data Subject Requests: Handling data subject requests in the context of OSINT can be challenging, particularly when individuals request access to or deletion of data that was collected from public sources. Organizations must have processes in place to verify the identity of the requester, determine whether the data is subject to legal exemptions, and respond to requests in a timely and compliant manner.

4. Best Practices for Complying with Data Protection Laws in OSINT

Conducting Data Protection Impact Assessments (DPIAs): DPIAs are a key tool for identifying and mitigating risks associated with data processing activities. OSINT practitioners should conduct DPIAs for any projects involving the collection or processing of personal data, particularly when dealing with large-scale data collection, sensitive data, or high-risk activities. DPIAs help organizations identify potential legal and ethical issues and implement appropriate safeguards.

Implementing Privacy by Design and Default: Privacy by design and default is a principle that requires organizations to build privacy protections into their systems and processes from the outset. For OSINT, this means designing tools and workflows that minimize data collection, protect data at all stages of processing, and ensure that privacy considerations are integrated into every aspect of the intelligence process.

Developing Clear Data Governance Policies: Organizations engaged in OSINT should develop clear data governance policies that outline how personal data will be collected, processed, stored, and shared. These policies should address key issues such as data retention, data access controls, and incident response procedures. Clear governance policies help ensure that OSINT activities are conducted in a manner that complies with data protection laws and protects individual rights.

Training and Awareness: Ensuring that all personnel involved in OSINT activities are aware of data protection laws and their responsibilities is crucial for compliance. Regular training sessions, workshops, and updates on legal developments can help build a culture of privacy and ensure that data protection principles are understood and applied in practice.

Engaging with Legal and Compliance Teams: OSINT practitioners should work closely with legal and compliance teams to ensure that their activities align with data protection laws. Legal teams can provide valuable guidance on complex legal issues, help navigate cross-jurisdictional challenges, and ensure that data protection considerations are integrated into OSINT operations.

Data protection laws play a critical role in shaping how OSINT activities are conducted, ensuring that personal data is handled responsibly and with respect for individual rights. While complying with these laws presents challenges, particularly in the context of global operations and cybersecurity investigations, organizations can navigate these complexities by adopting best practices, conducting thorough assessments, and fostering a culture of privacy. By aligning their OSINT activities with data protection laws, organizations can not only achieve compliance but also build trust with the individuals and communities they serve.

8.4. Compliance Challenges in Using AI for OSINT

The integration of Artificial Intelligence (AI) into Open Source Intelligence (OSINT) has revolutionized the field by enabling faster, more accurate, and more comprehensive analysis of vast amounts of data. However, the use of AI in OSINT also presents significant compliance challenges, particularly in relation to data protection laws, ethical considerations, and regulatory requirements. This section delves into the complexities and challenges of ensuring compliance when deploying AI technologies for OSINT, highlighting the need for a careful and strategic approach.

1. Legal and Regulatory Compliance Challenges

Adhering to Data Protection Laws: AI systems used in OSINT often process large volumes of personal data, which must comply with stringent data protection regulations such as the General Data Protection Regulation (GDPR) in the EU, the California Consumer Privacy Act (CCPA) in the US, and others globally. These laws require that personal data be processed lawfully, fairly, and transparently, with specific attention to the principles of data minimization, purpose limitation, and the rights of data subjects. The challenge lies in ensuring that AI-driven OSINT systems, which may automatically collect and analyze data, operate within these legal frameworks. For example, ensuring transparency in AI decisions and obtaining valid consent for data processing can be difficult when the data is sourced from publicly available information.

Cross-Border Data Transfers: OSINT operations often involve the collection and analysis of data from multiple countries, each with its own data protection laws. AI systems processing this data must navigate the complexities of cross-border data transfers, ensuring compliance with restrictions imposed by different jurisdictions. For instance, the GDPR imposes strict rules on the transfer of personal data outside the European Economic Area (EEA), requiring adequate safeguards such as Standard Contractual Clauses (SCCs) or Binding Corporate Rules (BCRs). Ensuring that AI systems comply with these requirements, especially when data is being processed in real-time across multiple locations, is a significant challenge.

Algorithmic Transparency and Explainability: Many AI algorithms, particularly those based on deep learning, are often described as "black boxes" due to their complexity and lack of transparency. This lack of transparency can be a significant compliance issue, especially under regulations that require explainability in automated decision-making processes. For instance, the GDPR mandates that individuals have the right to understand and challenge decisions made by AI systems that affect them. In the context of OSINT, where AI may be used to flag potential threats or identify persons of interest, the ability to explain how these conclusions were reached is crucial for legal and ethical compliance.

2. Ethical and Privacy Considerations

Ensuring Ethical Use of AI in OSINT: The use of AI in OSINT raises several ethical issues, particularly related to privacy, surveillance, and the potential for misuse of data. AI systems can inadvertently exacerbate biases in data, leading to unfair or discriminatory outcomes. For instance, if an AI system used for OSINT is trained on biased data, it may produce biased results, such as unfairly targeting certain groups or individuals. Ensuring that AI systems are designed and used ethically, with mechanisms in place to identify and mitigate bias, is a critical compliance challenge.

Balancing Privacy with Security Needs: OSINT often involves the collection of data from social media, forums, and other online platforms, which may include sensitive personal information. AI systems can enhance the efficiency and scope of this data collection, but they also increase the risk of infringing on individuals' privacy. The challenge is to balance the need for comprehensive threat intelligence with the obligation to respect privacy rights. This is particularly difficult in cases where the boundaries between public and private information are blurred, such as in social media posts that may be publicly accessible but still considered private by users.

Mitigating the Risk of AI Misuse: AI systems can be powerful tools for OSINT, but they can also be misused, either intentionally or unintentionally. For example, AI-driven OSINT tools could be used to gather information on individuals for malicious purposes, such as harassment or discrimination. Ensuring that AI tools are used responsibly, with strict controls and oversight to prevent misuse, is a key compliance challenge. This includes implementing policies and procedures that govern the use of AI in OSINT, as well as regular audits and monitoring to detect and address any instances of misuse.

3. Technical Challenges in Compliance

Data Quality and Integrity: AI systems rely on high-quality data to function effectively. In the context of OSINT, the data collected from various sources may be incomplete, inaccurate, or outdated, leading to potential compliance issues. Poor data quality can result in incorrect analysis, biased outcomes, or false positives, all of which can have legal and ethical implications. Ensuring that AI systems used in OSINT are fed with accurate and reliable data, and that there are mechanisms in place to validate and verify this data, is a significant challenge.

Implementing Data Anonymization and Pseudonymization: Data protection laws often require that personal data be anonymized or pseudonymized to protect individual privacy. However, in the context of AI-driven OSINT, achieving effective anonymization can be difficult, especially when dealing with large datasets that may be re-identified through sophisticated analysis techniques. Ensuring compliance with these requirements while maintaining the usefulness of the data for OSINT purposes is a complex technical challenge. Organizations must invest in advanced anonymization techniques and ensure that these are applied consistently across all AI systems.

Maintaining Auditability and Traceability: Compliance with data protection laws often requires organizations to demonstrate that their AI systems are operating in accordance with legal and regulatory requirements. This necessitates maintaining detailed records of data processing activities, including how data is collected, processed, and used by AI systems. The challenge lies in ensuring that AI-driven OSINT systems are auditable and that there is a clear traceability of data flows and decisions made by AI algorithms. This is particularly important in the event of a data breach or legal challenge, where organizations may need to provide evidence of compliance.

4. Organizational and Governance Challenges

Integrating AI into Existing Compliance Frameworks: Many organizations already have established compliance frameworks for handling data protection and privacy issues. Integrating AI-driven OSINT into these frameworks can be challenging, particularly when AI introduces new risks and complexities that were not previously accounted for. Organizations need to adapt their compliance strategies to address the specific challenges posed by AI, including updating policies, training staff, and implementing new oversight mechanisms.

Training and Awareness: Ensuring that all personnel involved in AI-driven OSINT are aware of the legal, ethical, and technical challenges is critical for compliance. This includes not only technical staff but also legal, compliance, and governance teams. Providing regular training and updates on the evolving regulatory landscape, as well as the specific risks associated with AI, is essential for building a culture of compliance and ensuring that all stakeholders are equipped to address these challenges effectively.

Managing Third-Party Risks: Many organizations rely on third-party vendors or partners to provide AI tools or data for OSINT purposes. Ensuring that these third parties comply with relevant data protection laws and ethical standards is a significant challenge. Organizations must conduct thorough due diligence on their third-party providers, including reviewing their data handling practices, security measures, and compliance with legal and regulatory requirements. Additionally, contracts with third-party providers should include specific provisions that address compliance and liability issues related to the use of AI in OSINT.

The use of AI in OSINTpresents a range of compliance challenges that span legal, ethical, technical, and organizational domains. Ensuring that AI-driven OSINT activities comply with data protection laws, ethical standards, and regulatory requirements requires a comprehensive and proactive approach. Organizations must invest in robust compliance frameworks, advanced technical solutions, and continuous training and awareness programs to navigate these challenges effectively. By addressing the compliance challenges associated with AI in OSINT, organizations can harness the power of AI while minimizing legal risks and ensuring that their activities are conducted responsibly and ethically.

8.5. Best Practices for Legal and Ethical Compliance

The rapid integration of Artificial Intelligence (AI) into Open Source Intelligence (OSINT) has transformed the landscape of cyber investigations, offering unprecedented capabilities in data collection, analysis, and threat detection. However, these advancements also bring about significant legal and ethical challenges. To navigate these challenges effectively, organizations must adopt best practices that ensure compliance with laws, regulations, and ethical standards. This section outlines key strategies for achieving legal and ethical compliance in the use of AI for OSINT.

1. Establishing a Comprehensive Compliance Framework

Develop Clear Policies and Procedures: Organizations should create detailed policies and procedures that govern the use of AI in OSINT activities. These documents should outline the legal and ethical standards that must be adhered to, including data protection, privacy, and non-discrimination. Policies should be regularly updated to reflect changes in the regulatory environment and advancements in AI technology.

Implement a Governance Structure: Establishing a robust governance structure is critical for ensuring compliance. This includes appointing dedicated compliance officers or committees responsible for overseeing AI-driven OSINT activities. These governance bodies should have the authority to enforce policies, conduct audits, and ensure that all AI applications align with legal and ethical standards.

Conduct Regular Compliance Audits: Regular audits are essential to identify potential compliance gaps and areas for improvement. Audits should cover all aspects of AI-driven OSINT, including data collection, processing, storage, and analysis. Organizations should also assess the effectiveness of their compliance policies and governance structures during these audits.

2. Ensuring Transparency and Accountability

Promote Algorithmic Transparency: One of the key challenges in AI is the opacity of algorithms, especially in complex systems like deep learning models. Organizations should strive for transparency by documenting how AI systems function, what data they use, and how decisions are made. This transparency is crucial for demonstrating compliance with regulations that require explainability in automated decision-making processes.

Maintain Detailed Records and Documentation: Keeping comprehensive records of all AI-driven OSINT activities is vital for legal and ethical compliance. This includes logs of data sources, processing methods, and the outcomes of AI analyses. Documentation should also include the rationale behind the use of specific AI models and how they are trained, tested, and validated. These records are invaluable in the event of a compliance audit or legal challenge.

Establish Accountability Mechanisms: Accountability is a cornerstone of ethical AI use. Organizations should implement mechanisms to ensure that individuals or teams are held accountable for the outcomes of AI-driven OSINT activities. This includes setting up processes for monitoring AI systems, reporting issues, and addressing any identified risks or breaches of compliance.

3. Protecting Privacy and Ensuring Ethical Use

Adopt Privacy-By-Design Principles: Privacy should be a core consideration in the design and deployment of AI systems for OSINT. Organizations should implement Privacy-By-Design principles, which involve embedding privacy protections into the AI system's architecture from the outset. This includes minimizing data collection, using anonymization or pseudonymization techniques, and ensuring that data is only used for its intended purpose.

Implement Ethical AI Practices: Ethical considerations should guide the development and use of AI in OSINT. Organizations must ensure that their AI systems do not perpetuate biases, discrimination, or other unethical practices. This can be achieved by conducting regular bias assessments, involving diverse teams in AI development, and adhering to ethical guidelines such as fairness, transparency, and accountability.

Obtain Informed Consent Where Applicable: In cases where AI-driven OSINT involves the processing of personal data, organizations should seek informed consent from individuals whenever possible. This includes providing clear and accessible information about how data will be used, the purpose of processing, and individuals' rights regarding their data. In situations where consent is not feasible, organizations must ensure that data processing is justified under other legal bases, such as legitimate interest or public interest.

4. Navigating Legal and Regulatory Requirements

Stay Informed of Regulatory Changes: The legal landscape surrounding AI and OSINT is constantly evolving. Organizations must stay informed of new laws, regulations, and guidelines that impact their use of AI. This includes monitoring developments in data protection laws, AI-specific regulations, and sector-specific rules, such as those related to cybersecurity and law enforcement.

Engage Legal Experts and Compliance Professionals: Given the complexity of legal and regulatory requirements, organizations should engage legal experts and compliance professionals with specific knowledge of AI and OSINT. These experts can provide guidance on navigating legal challenges, interpreting regulations, and implementing compliance strategies that align with the organization's goals.

Ensure Cross-Border Compliance: AI-driven OSINT often involves data collection and analysis across multiple jurisdictions, each with its own legal requirements. Organizations must ensure that their AI systems comply with the data protection and privacy laws of all relevant jurisdictions. This includes understanding the requirements for cross-border data transfers and implementing appropriate safeguards, such as Standard Contractual Clauses (SCCs) or Binding Corporate Rules (BCRs).

5. Building a Culture of Compliance and Ethics

Provide Training and Education: Ensuring that all employees, particularly those involved in AI and OSINT activities, are aware of legal and ethical compliance requirements is crucial. Organizations should offer regular training sessions on topics such as data protection laws, ethical AI practices, and the responsible use of OSINT. Training should be tailored to the specific roles and responsibilities of employees.

Foster Ethical Awareness: Beyond formal training, organizations should foster a culture of ethical awareness where employees are encouraged to consider the ethical implications of their work. This can be achieved through open discussions, workshops, and ethical review boards that provide a platform for addressing ethical dilemmas related to AI and OSINT.

Encourage Whistleblowing and Reporting of Concerns: Organizations should establish channels for employees to report concerns or violations related to AI-driven OSINT activities. Whistleblowing mechanisms should be confidential and protect employees from retaliation. Encouraging the reporting of concerns helps organizations identify and address potential compliance issues before they escalate.

6. Implementing Technical Safeguards

Use Data Anonymization and Pseudonymization: To protect privacy and comply with data protection laws, organizations should implement data anonymization and pseudonymization techniques. These techniques reduce the risk of re-identification of individuals in datasets used for OSINT. Organizations should ensure that these techniques are applied consistently and reviewed regularly to address any potential weaknesses.

Ensure Robust Security Measures: AI-driven OSINT systems must be secured against cyber threats to prevent unauthorized access, data breaches, and other security incidents. Organizations should implement robust security measures, including encryption, access controls, and regular security audits. Additionally, incident response plans should be in place to address any security breaches swiftly and effectively.

Conduct Regular Risk Assessments: Regular risk assessments are essential for identifying and mitigating potential legal, ethical, and technical risks associated with AI-driven OSINT. These assessments should evaluate the entire AI lifecycle, from data collection and model development to deployment and monitoring. Organizations should update their risk management strategies based on the findings of these assessments.

Achieving legal and ethical compliance in the use of AI for OSINT requires a multifaceted approach that encompasses governance, transparency, privacy, ethics, and technical safeguards. By adopting best practices in these areas, organizations can harness the power of AI while minimizing risks and ensuring that their OSINT activities align with legal and ethical standards. In a rapidly evolving regulatory landscape, staying proactive and vigilant in compliance efforts is essential for maintaining trust, protecting privacy, and upholding the integrity of AI-driven OSINT operations.

Chapter 9: Case Studies: AI in Action

Chapter 9, "Case Studies: AI in Action," presents a series of real-world examples that illustrate the practical application of Artificial Intelligence (AI) in Open Source Intelligence (OSINT) operations. This chapter details various successful and challenging AI-driven investigations, highlighting how AI tools and techniques have been employed to address complex cyber threats. Through these case studies, readers will gain insights into the tangible benefits and potential pitfalls of using AI in OSINT, learning from both effective implementations and lessons learned from less successful endeavors. This exploration of practical applications underscores the transformative impact of AI on cyber investigations and offers valuable takeaways for professionals in the field.

9.1. AI-Enhanced OSINT in Corporate Investigations

The integration of Artificial Intelligence (AI) into Open Source Intelligence (OSINT) has brought transformative changes to the field of corporate investigations. Companies are increasingly relying on AI-driven OSINT tools to conduct thorough, efficient, and accurate investigations into various corporate activities, such as fraud detection, intellectual property theft, employee misconduct, and competitive intelligence. This section explores how AI enhances OSINT in corporate investigations, offering both a strategic advantage and addressing challenges that arise in the process.

1. The Role of AI in Corporate Investigations

Automating Data Collection: Traditional OSINT methods require investigators to manually sift through vast amounts of information from publicly available sources, such as social media, news articles, financial records, and regulatory filings. AI-enhanced OSINT tools can automate this process, rapidly collecting and organizing relevant data from multiple sources. Machine learning algorithms can be trained to identify key information, reducing the time and effort required for data collection and enabling investigators to focus on analysis and decision-making.

Enhanced Data Analysis: AI-powered analytics enable investigators to process and analyze large datasets that would be overwhelming to handle manually. Advanced AI techniques, such as natural language processing (NLP) and sentiment analysis, allow for the interpretation of unstructured data, including text, images, and videos. For instance, NLP can analyze communication patterns in emails or social media posts to detect anomalies or signs of insider threats. AI can also identify patterns and correlations in data that might not be immediately apparent to human investigators, providing deeper insights into corporate activities.

Real-Time Monitoring and Alerts: AI-enhanced OSINT tools can continuously monitor specific data sources in real-time, providing alerts when significant changes or activities are detected. For example, AI systems can track social media mentions of a company or monitor financial transactions for unusual activity. This capability is particularly valuable in corporate investigations where timely information is critical, such as during a merger or acquisition, or in response to an emerging crisis. Real-time monitoring allows companies to respond quickly to potential threats or issues, mitigating risks before they escalate.

Risk Assessment and Predictive Analytics: AI's predictive capabilities are a game-changer in corporate investigations. By analyzing historical data and identifying trends, AI can help predict potential risks or future developments. For example, AI can assess the likelihood of financial fraud by analyzing patterns in transaction data or predict the impact of a new competitor entering the market by examining market trends and consumer sentiment. These insights enable companies to take proactive measures to protect their interests and maintain a competitive edge.

2. Key Applications of AI-Enhanced OSINT in Corporate Investigations

Fraud Detection and Prevention: Fraud is a significant concern for many corporations, and AI-enhanced OSINT tools are increasingly used to detect and prevent fraudulent activities. AI can analyze financial records, transactional data, and communication logs to identify suspicious behavior or anomalies that may indicate fraud. For instance, AI can detect patterns of unusual spending, duplicate transactions, or inconsistent reporting that could signal financial misconduct. By automating these processes, companies can more effectively identify and address fraud, reducing losses and protecting their assets.

Intellectual Property Protection: Protecting intellectual property (IP) is crucial for many businesses, especially in industries like technology, pharmaceuticals, and entertainment. AI-enhanced OSINT can monitor online platforms, marketplaces, and social media for unauthorized use or distribution of a company's IP. For example, AI tools can detect counterfeit products being sold online or track the unauthorized sharing of copyrighted material. By identifying these activities early, companies can take swift legal action to protect their IP and minimize financial losses.

Employee and Insider Threat Investigations: Internal threats, whether intentional or accidental, can pose significant risks to a company's security and reputation. AI-enhanced OSINT can monitor employee behavior across various platforms, such as email, social media, and internal communication tools, to identify potential insider threats. For example, AI can analyze communication patterns to detect signs of disgruntlement or attempts to leak confidential information. By proactively identifying and addressing insider threats, companies can safeguard their sensitive data and maintain a secure working environment.

Competitive Intelligence: Understanding the competitive landscape is vital for strategic decision-making in any business. AI-enhanced OSINT tools can gather and analyze data on competitors, including their financial performance, marketing strategies, and customer sentiment. AI can track competitors' online activities, such as product launches, partnerships, and media coverage, providing companies with valuable insights to inform their strategies. Additionally, AI's predictive analytics can help forecast competitors' future actions, enabling companies to stay ahead in the market.

3. Challenges in Implementing AI-Enhanced OSINT for Corporate Investigations

Data Privacy and Compliance Issues: One of the primary challenges in using AI-enhanced OSINT for corporate investigations is navigating data privacy and compliance regulations. Companies must ensure that their data collection and analysis practices comply with laws such as the General Data Protection Regulation (GDPR) and the California Consumer Privacy Act (CCPA). This includes obtaining the necessary consents, protecting personal data, and ensuring transparency in data processing. Failure to comply with these regulations can result in legal penalties and damage to a company's reputation.

Managing False Positives and Biases: While AI can significantly enhance the efficiency of OSINT, it is not infallible. AI algorithms can produce false positives, flagging innocent behavior as suspicious, or be biased due to the data they are trained on. This can lead to incorrect conclusions and potentially harm individuals or the company. It is essential for companies to implement robust validation processes, involve human oversight in the analysis, and continuously monitor and update AI models to reduce the risk of errors and biases.

Cost and Resource Allocation: Implementing AI-enhanced OSINT tools can be resource-intensive, requiring significant investment in technology, personnel, and training. Companies must weigh the costs against the benefits, considering factors such as the scale of their operations, the complexity of the investigations, and the potential return on investment. Additionally, integrating AI tools with existing systems and workflows can be challenging, requiring careful planning and coordination.

Ethical Considerations: The use of AI in corporate investigations raises ethical questions, particularly related to privacy, surveillance, and the potential for misuse. Companies must consider the ethical implications of their AI-driven OSINT activities, ensuring that they respect individuals' rights and do not engage in unjust or discriminatory practices. Establishing clear ethical guidelines and fostering a culture of responsibility is crucial for maintaining the integrity of corporate investigations.

4. Best Practices for Leveraging AI-Enhanced OSINT in Corporate Investigations

Integrate Human Expertise with AI: While AI offers powerful capabilities, human expertise remains essential in corporate investigations. Companies should combine AI-driven insights with the experience and judgment of skilled investigators to ensure accurate and reliable outcomes. Human oversight is particularly important in interpreting AI-generated data, validating findings, and making strategic decisions.

Ensure Continuous Monitoring and Improvement: AI and OSINT tools should be continuously monitored and updated to adapt to new threats, changes in the regulatory environment, and advancements in technology. Regularly reviewing and improving AI models, data sources, and analysis methods is critical for maintaining the effectiveness and compliance of corporate investigations.

Prioritize Ethical and Legal Compliance: Compliance with legal and ethical standards should be a top priority in any AI-enhanced OSINT activity. Companies should establish clear policies, provide training to employees, and engage legal and ethical experts to navigate the complexities of AI and OSINT. This proactive approach helps mitigate risks and ensures that investigations are conducted responsibly and within the bounds of the law.

Leverage AI for Strategic Decision-Making: Beyond its role in investigations, AI-enhanced OSINT can provide valuable insights for broader strategic decision-making. By leveraging AI to analyze market trends, competitive activities, and emerging threats, companies can make informed decisions that drive growth and protect their interests.

AI-enhanced OSINT is revolutionizing corporate investigations, offering powerful tools for detecting fraud, protecting intellectual property, managing insider threats, and gaining competitive intelligence. However, its implementation comes with challenges, including compliance with data privacy laws, managing biases, and addressing ethical concerns. By adopting best practices and integrating AI with human expertise, companies can harness the full potential of AI-enhanced OSINT to conduct effective and responsible corporate investigations, ultimately strengthening their position in the marketplace.

9.2. AI in Law Enforcement and Cybercrime Detection

The rise of cybercrime has posed significant challenges to law enforcement agencies worldwide, necessitating the adoption of advanced technologies to stay ahead of increasingly sophisticated threats. Artificial Intelligence (AI) has emerged as a critical tool in the fight against cybercrime, offering law enforcement agencies the ability to detect, prevent, and respond to criminal activities more efficiently and effectively. This section delves into the various ways AI is transforming law enforcement efforts in cybercrime detection, highlighting its capabilities, applications, challenges, and the ethical considerations involved.

1. The Role of AI in Cybercrime Detection

Automated Threat Detection and Analysis: Traditional methods of cybercrime detection often involve manual analysis of vast amounts of data, which can be time-consuming and prone to human error. AI, with its ability to process large datasets quickly and accurately, can automate threat detection, identifying patterns, anomalies, and indicators of compromise (IoCs) that may signal cybercriminal activities. Machine learning algorithms can analyze network traffic, user behavior, and system logs in real-time, providing early warnings of potential attacks and enabling swift responses.

Advanced Malware Detection: Cybercriminals continually evolve their tactics, developing new types of malware that can evade conventional detection methods. AI-driven systems can enhance malware detection by using techniques such as machine learning, deep learning, and behavioral analysis. These systems can recognize previously unknown malware variants by analyzing their behavior and comparing it to known malicious patterns. This proactive approach allows law enforcement agencies to detect and mitigate threats before they can cause significant damage.

Predictive Policing and Crime Prevention: AI's predictive capabilities are particularly valuable in law enforcement, where the ability to anticipate and prevent crimes is a top priority. By analyzing historical crime data, social media activity, and other relevant data sources, AI can identify trends and predict potential criminal hotspots or individuals at risk of committing cybercrimes. This information allows law enforcement agencies to allocate resources more effectively, focusing their efforts on high-risk areas and individuals, and preventing crimes before they occur.

Enhanced Digital Forensics: In the aftermath of a cybercrime, digital forensics plays a crucial role in identifying the perpetrators, understanding the scope of the attack, and gathering evidence for prosecution. AI can significantly enhance digital forensics by automating the analysis of large volumes of digital evidence, such as emails, chat logs, and files. AI-powered tools can sift through this data to identify relevant information, reconstruct the timeline of events, and link the evidence to specific individuals or groups, making the investigative process faster and more accurate.

2. Key Applications of AI in Law Enforcement for Cybercrime Detection

Facial Recognition and Biometrics: AI-powered facial recognition technology is increasingly used in law enforcement to identify and track suspects involved in cybercrimes. By analyzing video footage, images, and other biometric data, AI can match faces against criminal databases, flagging known offenders or persons of interest. This technology is particularly useful in cases involving identity theft, fraud, and cyberstalking, where the identification of the perpetrator is critical to the investigation.

Social Media Monitoring: Social media platforms are often used by cybercriminals to coordinate activities, recruit members, and disseminate malicious content. AI tools can monitor social media in real-time, analyzing posts, comments, and messages for signs of criminal intent or activity. Natural Language Processing (NLP) algorithms can detect keywords, phrases, and patterns indicative of cybercrime, enabling law enforcement to intervene before crimes are carried out. This capability is essential in combating online threats such as cyberbullying, hate speech, and terrorist activities.

Dark Web Surveillance: The dark web is a haven for cybercriminals, where illegal activities such as drug trafficking, weapons sales, and human trafficking are conducted anonymously. AI enhances law enforcement's ability to monitor and investigate the dark web by automating the identification of illegal marketplaces, forums, and communication channels. Machine learning algorithms can analyze the content of dark web pages, detect suspicious activities, and trace the origins of illicit transactions, helping law enforcement agencies disrupt criminal networks operating in the shadows.

AI in Cybersecurity Operations Centers (CSOCs): Many law enforcement agencies have established Cybersecurity Operations Centers (CSOCs) to monitor and respond to cyber threats in real-time. AI plays a crucial role in these centers by automating the detection of cyber threats, analyzing security alerts, and prioritizing responses based on the severity of the threat. AI-driven CSOCs can quickly identify and mitigate cyberattacks, reducing the time it takes to respond to incidents and minimizing the damage caused by cybercriminals.

3. Challenges and Ethical Considerations in AI-Driven Law Enforcement

Data Privacy and Surveillance Concerns: The use of AI in law enforcement, particularly for cybercrime detection, raises significant data privacy and surveillance concerns. AI systems often rely on large amounts of data, including personal information, to function effectively. However, the collection, storage, and analysis of this data can infringe on individuals' privacy rights. There is also the risk of over-surveillance, where AI-driven monitoring could lead to the unjust targeting of certain individuals or groups. Law enforcement agencies must strike a balance between effective crime detection and the protection of civil liberties, ensuring that their use of AI complies with legal and ethical standards.

Bias in AI Algorithms: AI systems are only as good as the data they are trained on. If the training data contains biases, these biases can be reflected in the AI's outputs, leading to discriminatory outcomes in law enforcement. For example, an AI system trained on biased crime data may disproportionately target certain racial or ethnic groups, perpetuating existing inequalities in the criminal justice system. Law enforcement agencies must be vigilant in assessing and mitigating biases in their AI systems, ensuring that their use of AI is fair, transparent, and non-discriminatory.

Reliability and Accuracy of AI Systems: While AI offers significant advantages in cybercrime detection, it is not infallible. AI systems can produce false positives, flagging innocent activities as suspicious, or false negatives, failing to detect actual criminal activities. These inaccuracies can have serious consequences, including wrongful arrests, missed threats, and undermined public trust in law enforcement. To address these challenges, law enforcement agencies must implement rigorous testing, validation, and oversight processes to ensure the reliability and accuracy of their AI systems.

Legal and Regulatory Challenges: The use of AI in law enforcement is subject to a complex and evolving legal and regulatory landscape. Different jurisdictions have different laws governing the use of AI, data privacy, and surveillance, creating challenges for law enforcement agencies operating across borders. Additionally, the legal framework surrounding AI is still developing, with many unanswered questions about accountability, liability, and the admissibility of AI-generated evidence in court.

Law enforcement agencies must stay informed of legal developments and work closely with legal experts to navigate these challenges.

4. Best Practices for Implementing AI in Cybercrime Detection

Adopt a Human-in-the-Loop Approach: While AI can automate many aspects of cybercrime detection, human judgment remains essential in the decision-making process. Law enforcement agencies should adopt a human-in-the-loop approach, where AI systems assist human officers rather than replace them. This approach ensures that AI-generated insights are carefully evaluated, reducing the risk of errors and ensuring that decisions are made with consideration of all relevant factors.

Ensure Transparency and Accountability: Transparency is crucial in maintaining public trust in the use of AI for law enforcement. Agencies should be transparent about how AI systems are used, what data they rely on, and how decisions are made. Additionally, there should be clear accountability mechanisms in place to address any errors or abuses of AI technology. This includes regular audits, the establishment of oversight bodies, and the provision of avenues for public feedback and redress.

Invest in Training and Education: The successful implementation of AI in cybercrime detection requires a skilled and knowledgeable workforce. Law enforcement agencies should invest in training and education for their officers, ensuring they understand how AI systems work, how to interpret AI-generated insights, and how to address potential challenges. Continuous learning is essential, given the rapid pace of AI advancements and the evolving nature of cyber threats.

Collaborate with Industry and Academia: Collaboration between law enforcement, industry, and academia is key to advancing the use of AI in cybercrime detection. Industry partners can provide access to cutting-edge AI technologies and expertise, while academic institutions can contribute research and insights into the ethical, legal, and technical aspects of AI. By working together, these stakeholders can develop innovative solutions, share best practices, and address common challenges in the fight against cybercrime.

AI has become an indispensable tool in law enforcement's efforts to detect and combat cybercrime. From automating threat detection and enhancing digital forensics to monitoring social media and the dark web, AI offers law enforcement agencies powerful capabilities to stay ahead of cybercriminals. However, the implementation of AI in cybercrime detection comes with challenges, including data privacy concerns, biases in AI algorithms, and legal complexities. By adopting best practices, such as ensuring transparency, integrating human expertise, and investing in training, law enforcement agencies can harness the full potential of AI while addressing these challenges responsibly. As cyber threats continue to evolve, the role of AI in law enforcement will only become more critical, shaping the future of cybercrime detection and prevention.

9.3. Successful AI-Driven Investigations in Cybersecurity

In recent years, Artificial Intelligence (AI) has revolutionized the field of cybersecurity, offering unprecedented capabilities for detecting, analyzing, and responding to cyber threats. This section explores several case studies that showcase the success of AI-driven investigations in cybersecurity. These examples highlight how AI has been leveraged to uncover complex cyber threats, enhance the efficiency and accuracy of investigations, and ultimately strengthen the defenses of organizations against increasingly sophisticated adversaries.

1. Case Study 1: Unraveling a Complex Phishing Campaign

Background:

A major financial institution was targeted by a highly sophisticated phishing campaign designed to steal sensitive customer information. The attackers used advanced social engineering tactics and meticulously crafted emails that closely mimicked the institution's official communications.

AI Involvement:

The cybersecurity team deployed an AI-powered email security system that used machine learning algorithms to analyze incoming emails in real-time. The system was trained on a vast dataset of known phishing emails, enabling it to detect subtle indicators of phishing, such as slight variations in domain names, abnormal patterns in email metadata, and the use of persuasive language typical of phishing attempts.

Outcome:

The AI system successfully identified the phishing emails before they reached customers, preventing any data breaches. Further analysis by the AI system revealed a network of interconnected phishing campaigns targeting other financial institutions. The investigation led to the identification and dismantling of the cybercriminal group responsible for the attacks. This case demonstrated how AI can enhance the speed and accuracy of threat detection, enabling proactive defenses against phishing and other social engineering attacks.

2. Case Study 2: Detecting Insider Threats with AI

Background:

A multinational technology company suspected that sensitive intellectual property (IP) was being leaked to competitors. Traditional security measures failed to identify any clear evidence of an insider threat, leading to concerns about the company's ability to protect its assets.

AI Involvement:

The company implemented an AI-driven insider threat detection system that monitored employee behavior and data access patterns across the organization. The system used machine learning algorithms to establish baselines of normal behavior for each employee and detect deviations that could indicate malicious intent. Additionally, the system employed natural language processing (NLP) to analyze internal communications for signs of disgruntlement, intent to leak information, or unauthorized data sharing.

Outcome:

The AI system detected unusual access patterns from an employee who was attempting to download large amounts of sensitive data outside of their normal work hours. Further investigation revealed that the employee had been in contact with a competitor and was planning to leak the company's IP. The AI-driven investigation provided the evidence needed to prevent the leak, and the employee was terminated. This case highlights the effectiveness of AI in identifying insider threats that might otherwise go unnoticed by traditional security measures.

3. Case Study 3: AI in Threat Hunting and Malware Analysis

Background:

A government agency responsible for national security was targeted by a series of advanced persistent threat (APT) attacks. The attackers used custom malware that evaded detection by traditional antivirus solutions, raising concerns about the agency's ability to defend against sophisticated threats.

AI Involvement:

The agency deployed an AI-powered threat-hunting platform that specialized in advanced malware detection and analysis. The platform used deep learning algorithms to analyze file behaviors, network traffic, and system activities to identify previously unknown malware variants. The AI system also included a sandbox environment where suspicious files could be executed and observed in a controlled setting, allowing for detailed analysis of their behavior.

Outcome:

The AI platform successfully identified several instances of the custom malware that had infiltrated the agency's network. The detailed analysis provided by the AI system enabled the cybersecurity team to understand the malware's functionality, including its communication methods and payload delivery mechanisms. This information was crucial in developing effective countermeasures and patching vulnerabilities exploited by the attackers. The AI-driven investigation not only neutralized the immediate threat but also enhanced the agency's overall resilience against future APT attacks.

4. Case Study 4: AI in Supply Chain Security

Background:

A global manufacturing firm experienced a significant cyberattack that disrupted its supply chain operations. The attack involved ransomware that encrypted critical data, halting production and threatening the company's ability to fulfill orders.

AI Involvement:

The firm employed an AI-based cybersecurity solution designed to monitor and protect the supply chain. The AI system analyzed data from various sources, including vendor communications, shipment logs, and network traffic, to detect anomalies that could indicate cyber threats. The system's predictive analytics capabilities allowed it to identify potential vulnerabilities in the supply chain before they could be exploited by attackers.

Outcome:

The AI system detected unusual activity in a vendor's network, which was later confirmed to be the entry point for the ransomware attack. By identifying the compromised vendor early, the firm was able to isolate the threat and prevent it from spreading further within its network. The AI-driven investigation also provided insights into the attackers' methods, leading to the implementation of stronger security measures across the supply chain. This case illustrates the importance of AI in securing complex, interconnected networks like supply chains, where a single vulnerability can have widespread consequences.

5. Case Study 5: AI in Identifying Fraudulent Transactions

Background:

A major e-commerce platform was facing a surge in fraudulent transactions, resulting in significant financial losses and damage to its reputation. The traditional fraud detection systems were struggling to keep up with the rapidly evolving tactics used by fraudsters.

AI Involvement:

The platform integrated an AI-driven fraud detection system that utilized machine learning to analyze transaction data in real-time. The AI system was capable of learning from each transaction, continuously refining its models to identify fraudulent activities with greater accuracy. It analyzed various factors, such as transaction amounts, user behavior, IP addresses, and payment methods, to detect patterns indicative of fraud.

Outcome:

The AI system quickly identified and blocked numerous fraudulent transactions, significantly reducing the platform's financial losses. In addition to real-time detection, the AI system's insights into the fraudsters' tactics enabled the platform to strengthen its security protocols and reduce future vulnerabilities. The success of this AI-driven investigation underscored the critical role of AI in combating financial fraud in fast-paced digital environments.

These case studies demonstrate the transformative impact of AI on cybersecurity investigations. From detecting sophisticated phishing campaigns to uncovering insider threats, AI has proven its value as a powerful tool in the fight against cybercrime. By automating complex tasks, enhancing threat detection, and providing actionable insights, AI has enabled organizations to respond more effectively to cyber threats and protect their critical assets. As cyber threats continue to evolve, the importance of AI-driven investigations in cybersecurity will only grow, making AI an indispensable part of any modern security strategy.

9.4. Lessons from Failed AI-OSINT Initiatives

The integration of Artificial Intelligence (AI) with Open Source Intelligence (OSINT) has the potential to revolutionize cyber investigations by providing enhanced capabilities for data analysis, threat detection, and decision-making. However, not all AI-OSINT initiatives have been successful. Some have faced significant challenges, resulting in underperformance or outright failure. Understanding the reasons behind these failures is crucial for improving future implementations. This section explores several failed AI-OSINT initiatives, analyzing the factors that led to their downfall and drawing lessons that can inform the development of more effective solutions.

1. Case Study 1: Overreliance on AI with Insufficient Human Oversight

Background:

A large government agency implemented an AI-OSINT platform to automate the collection and analysis of vast amounts of public data for national security purposes. The goal was to streamline operations and reduce the workload on analysts by allowing AI to make initial assessments and flag potential threats.

What Went Wrong:

The agency overestimated the AI system's capabilities and underestimated the need for human oversight. The AI platform was given too much autonomy, leading to several false positives and false negatives in threat detection. The system flagged benign activities as potential threats, causing unnecessary investigations and straining resources. Conversely, it missed significant indicators of actual threats, which later escalated into serious security incidents. The lack of human involvement in reviewing and validating the AI's findings was a critical factor in the failure.

Lessons Learned:

- **Balance AI with Human Expertise**: AI should complement, not replace, human judgment. Ensuring that AI-driven systems are used alongside skilled analysts who can interpret and validate AI findings is essential to prevent errors and improve accuracy.
- **Implement a Human-in-the-Loop System**: Continuous human oversight, particularly in critical decision-making processes, is vital. This approach allows

for a balance between AI's efficiency and the nuanced understanding that only humans can provide.

2. Case Study 2: Inadequate Training Data and Algorithm Bias

Background:

A private cybersecurity firm developed an AI-OSINT tool designed to identify emerging cyber threats by analyzing social media and online forums. The system relied on machine learning algorithms trained on historical data to detect patterns and predict future threats.

What Went Wrong:

The training data used to develop the AI model was biased and not representative of the diverse and evolving nature of online content. As a result, the AI system developed a skewed understanding of what constituted a threat. It disproportionately flagged content from certain demographics while missing actual threats from other groups. This not only led to inaccurate threat detection but also raised ethical concerns regarding the biased targeting of specific communities.

Lessons Learned:

- **Ensure Diverse and Representative Training Data**: The quality and diversity of training data are crucial for the success of AI systems. Training datasets must be carefully curated to represent the full spectrum of potential scenarios, minimizing the risk of bias.
- **Regularly Update and Validate Models**: AI models should be continuously updated with new data and regularly validated against real-world outcomes to ensure they remain accurate and unbiased.

3. Case Study 3: Failure to Address Data Privacy Concerns

Background:

A tech company launched an AI-OSINT platform intended to help businesses monitor and analyze publicly available data about their competitors. The tool provided insights into market trends, consumer sentiment, and competitor strategies.

What Went Wrong:

The AI platform faced backlash due to its invasive data collection methods, which were perceived as violating individuals' privacy rights. The system collected and analyzed personal data from social media profiles, online reviews, and other sources without adequate anonymization or user consent. This led to public outcry and legal challenges, ultimately forcing the company to shut down the platform.

Lessons Learned:

- **Prioritize Data Privacy and Compliance**: AI-OSINT initiatives must adhere to data privacy laws and ethical standards. This includes ensuring that data is collected, stored, and analyzed in a way that respects individuals' privacy rights and complies with relevant regulations.
- **Implement Robust Data Anonymization Techniques**: To protect user privacy, AI systems should employ anonymization techniques that remove or obscure personally identifiable information (PII) before data is processed.

4. Case Study 4: Overcomplexity and Lack of User Adoption

Background:

A multinational corporation developed an AI-OSINT platform to enhance its internal cybersecurity capabilities. The platform was designed with advanced features, including real-time threat monitoring, automated reporting, and integration with other security tools.

What Went Wrong:

Despite its technical sophistication, the platform was too complex for the intended users, who found it difficult to navigate and utilize effectively. The system required extensive training and had a steep learning curve, which led to low user adoption rates. Many employees reverted to using simpler, more familiar tools, rendering the AI-OSINT platform largely ineffective.

Lessons Learned:

- **Focus on Usability and User Experience**: The success of AI-OSINT tools depends not only on their technical capabilities but also on their usability. Tools should be intuitive, user-friendly, and designed with the end-users in mind to ensure widespread adoption and effective utilization.

- **Provide Adequate Training and Support**: Implementing AI-OSINT systems should be accompanied by comprehensive training and ongoing support to help users understand and leverage the tool's full capabilities.

5. Case Study 5: Insufficient Integration with Existing Systems

Background:

A financial services firm introduced an AI-OSINT tool to enhance its fraud detection capabilities. The tool was expected to integrate with the firm's existing security infrastructure and provide real-time insights into potential fraudulent activities.

What Went Wrong:

The AI-OSINT tool struggled to integrate seamlessly with the firm's legacy systems, leading to data silos, delayed reporting, and inconsistent results. The lack of compatibility hindered the flow of information between the AI tool and other security platforms, resulting in missed opportunities to detect and prevent fraud.

Lessons Learned:

- **Ensure Seamless Integration**: AI-OSINT tools should be compatible with existing systems and infrastructure to maximize their effectiveness. Integration challenges must be addressed during the planning phase to prevent operational disruptions.
- **Adopt a Phased Implementation Approach**: Gradually introducing AI-OSINT tools, with close monitoring of their integration with existing systems, can help identify and resolve issues before they escalate.

The failures of these AI-OSINT initiatives provide valuable insights into the challenges and pitfalls of integrating AI with OSINT. From the importance of balancing AI with human oversight to the need for diverse training data, these lessons emphasize the importance of careful planning, ethical considerations, and user-centric design in the development of AI-OSINT tools. By learning from past mistakes, organizations can better harness the power of AI in OSINT to achieve more successful and effective outcomes in the future.

9.5. Future Trends in AI and OSINT Case Applications

The integration of Artificial Intelligence (AI) with Open Source Intelligence (OSINT) is continually evolving, driven by advancements in technology and the ever-changing landscape of cyber threats. As AI technologies become more sophisticated and data sources more abundant, the applications of AI in OSINT are expected to grow in both scope and complexity. This section explores emerging trends and potential future applications of AI in OSINT, highlighting how these developments may shape the future of cyber investigations and intelligence gathering.

1. Enhanced Predictive Analytics

Trend:

AI's predictive capabilities are expected to become more advanced, enabling more accurate forecasting of future threats and vulnerabilities. By leveraging machine learning algorithms and vast datasets, AI systems will increasingly be able to predict cyber threats before they materialize.

Application:

For instance, AI could analyze historical data on cyber incidents, combined with real-time data from social media, forums, and dark web sources, to identify patterns and predict potential attacks. Organizations could use these predictions to implement proactive measures, such as strengthening defenses or altering security strategies to mitigate anticipated threats.

Example:

An AI-powered tool might predict a rise in ransomware attacks targeting specific industries based on emerging patterns in malware distribution and hacker communications. Organizations could then preemptively bolster their defenses and develop targeted incident response plans.

2. Integration of Multi-Modal Data Sources

Trend:

The future of AI-OSINT will likely involve the integration of multiple data sources, including text, images, video, and audio, to provide a more comprehensive view of potential threats. Advances in natural language processing (NLP) and computer vision will enable AI systems to analyze diverse types of data simultaneously.

Application:

AI systems could analyze social media posts, images from surveillance cameras, and voice data from public communications to detect coordinated threats or criminal activities. This multi-modal approach will enhance the accuracy of threat detection and provide more actionable intelligence.

Example:

During a security event, an AI system might correlate a social media post with an image of a suspicious package captured by a security camera, providing a more complete assessment of the situation and enabling a faster response.

3. Improved Real-Time Threat Detection

Trend:

AI's real-time processing capabilities are expected to improve, allowing for faster and more accurate detection of emerging threats. As AI algorithms become more efficient, they will be able to process and analyze data in real-time, reducing the time it takes to identify and respond to threats.

Application:

Real-time threat detection systems will become more adept at monitoring live data streams from various sources, including network traffic, social media, and dark web forums. This will enable organizations to respond to threats as they develop, rather than reacting to incidents after they occur.

Example:

An AI system might instantly flag unusual network activity associated with a zero-day exploit, triggering an automated response to contain the threat before it spreads.

4. Advanced Anomaly Detection

Trend:

AI-driven anomaly detection will continue to evolve, with improved algorithms capable of identifying subtle deviations from normal behavior. This will enhance the ability to detect sophisticated attacks that may otherwise go unnoticed by traditional security measures.

Application:

AI systems will be able to analyze vast amounts of data to identify anomalies that indicate potential threats, such as unusual patterns in user behavior or network traffic. This will help in detecting advanced persistent threats (APTs) and other complex cyber attacks.

Example:

An AI system might identify a slight deviation in the behavior of an employee's account, such as an unusual login time or access to sensitive data, which could indicate a compromised account or insider threat.

5. Enhanced Data Privacy and Security

Trend:

As AI and OSINT tools handle increasing amounts of sensitive information, there will be a greater emphasis on ensuring data privacy and security. Future developments will focus on incorporating advanced encryption techniques and privacy-preserving technologies.

Application:

AI systems will utilize techniques such as federated learning and homomorphic encryption to analyze data without exposing sensitive information. These approaches will help organizations comply with data protection regulations while still leveraging AI for intelligence gathering.

Example:

An AI-OSINT tool might use federated learning to train models on decentralized data sources, ensuring that individual data privacy is maintained while still improving the accuracy of threat detection.

6. Autonomous OSINT Platforms

Trend:

The development of autonomous OSINT platforms will enable AI systems to independently gather, analyze, and act on intelligence without human intervention. These platforms will be capable of self-learning and adapting to new threats and data sources.

Application:

Autonomous platforms could automatically monitor and analyze various data sources, generate intelligence reports, and even take actions such as issuing alerts or initiating defensive measures. This will increase the efficiency of intelligence operations and reduce the reliance on manual processes.

Example:

An autonomous OSINT platform might detect a new type of malware through online forums and automatically update security policies across an organization to protect against the newly identified threat.

7. Enhanced Collaboration and Data Sharing

Trend:

Future AI-OSINT applications will likely include enhanced collaboration and data-sharing capabilities, enabling different organizations and agencies to share intelligence and coordinate responses more effectively.

Application:

AI systems will facilitate secure data sharing and collaboration between organizations, enhancing collective cybersecurity efforts. This could involve sharing threat intelligence, attack indicators, and defensive strategies in real-time.

Example:

During a widespread cyber attack, AI systems from different organizations could share information about the attack's tactics and indicators, enabling a coordinated response and improving overall defense mechanisms.

8. Customizable and Adaptive AI Solutions

Trend:

AI-OSINT tools will become more customizable and adaptive, allowing organizations to tailor solutions to their specific needs and threats. This will involve developing AI systems that can be easily adjusted and configured based on organizational requirements and evolving threat landscapes.

Application:

Organizations will be able to customize AI-OSINT tools to focus on particular types of threats or data sources relevant to their operations. This flexibility will enhance the relevance and effectiveness of the intelligence gathered.

Example:

A financial institution might customize an AI-OSINT tool to prioritize monitoring for financial fraud indicators, while a healthcare organization might focus on detecting threats related to patient data breaches.

9. Integration with Emerging Technologies

Trend:

AI and OSINT will increasingly integrate with emerging technologies such as blockchain, Internet of Things (IoT), and 5G. These integrations will provide new opportunities for intelligence gathering and threat detection.

Application:

AI systems will leverage blockchain for secure data sharing, use IoT data for real-time threat monitoring, and analyze 5G network traffic for potential vulnerabilities. These integrations will enhance the overall effectiveness of AI-OSINT solutions.

Example:

AI might analyze data from IoT devices to detect anomalous behavior indicating a potential cyber attack, such as unauthorized access to a smart building system, and provide actionable intelligence for mitigating the threat.

10. Focus on Ethical AI and Responsible Use

Trend:

There will be a growing emphasis on the ethical use of AI in OSINT, including considerations for fairness, accountability, and transparency. Ensuring responsible use of AI technologies will be critical as their applications expand.

Application:

Organizations will implement ethical guidelines and frameworks for AI-OSINT tools to ensure they are used responsibly and transparently. This will include addressing concerns related to bias, privacy, and the potential misuse of technology.

Example:

An organization might develop an ethical AI framework that includes regular audits of AI-OSINT tools for bias and transparency, ensuring that the tools are used in a manner that respects privacy and upholds ethical standards.

The future of AI in OSINT holds exciting possibilities, with advancements poised to enhance predictive analytics, multi-modal data integration, and real-time threat detection. As AI technologies continue to evolve, they will offer new opportunities for more effective and efficient intelligence gathering. However, addressing challenges related to privacy, ethical considerations, and integration with existing systems will be crucial for ensuring the responsible and successful application of AI in OSINT. By staying abreast of these trends and continuously improving AI-OSINT tools, organizations can better prepare for and respond to the ever-evolving landscape of cyber threats.

Chapter 10: The Future of AI and OSINT

Chapter 10, "The Future of AI and OSINT," looks ahead to the evolving landscape of Artificial Intelligence (AI) and Open Source Intelligence (OSINT) and their potential future developments. This chapter explores emerging technologies and trends that are poised to shape the next generation of cyber investigations. It discusses anticipated advancements in AI capabilities, new methodologies in OSINT, and how these innovations might impact the field. By examining future possibilities and preparing for upcoming challenges, the chapter provides a forward-looking perspective on how AI and OSINT will continue to evolve and enhance the way we approach cybersecurity and intelligence gathering.

10.1. Emerging AI Technologies in OSINT

As the field of Artificial Intelligence (AI) continues to advance, several emerging technologies are poised to transform Open Source Intelligence (OSINT) practices. These innovations offer new capabilities for data collection, analysis, and threat detection, enhancing the overall effectiveness of intelligence operations. This section explores some of the most promising emerging AI technologies in OSINT and their potential applications.

1. Generative AI Models

Overview:

Generative AI models, including advanced techniques such as Generative Adversarial Networks (GANs) and Transformer-based models like GPT-4, are making significant strides in creating and analyzing data. These models can generate realistic text, images, and even videos, which can be useful for both intelligence gathering and understanding potential threats.

Applications in OSINT:

- **Content Generation**: Generative AI can create synthetic data to simulate various scenarios, helping analysts understand potential threats or prepare for different attack vectors.

- **Data Augmentation**: By generating additional data, these models can help enhance training datasets for other AI tools, improving their accuracy and effectiveness in threat detection.

Example:

A GAN could generate simulated phishing emails for training purposes, allowing cybersecurity teams to develop more robust phishing detection mechanisms.

2. Advanced Natural Language Processing (NLP)

Overview:

Recent advancements in NLP, driven by large-scale language models and deep learning techniques, are enhancing the ability to understand and process human language. This includes sentiment analysis, entity recognition, and context understanding, which are crucial for interpreting and analyzing vast amounts of text data.

Applications in OSINT:

- **Sentiment Analysis**: NLP can analyze social media posts, news articles, and other text sources to gauge public sentiment or detect emerging threats based on the emotional tone of communications.
- **Entity Recognition**: AI can identify and categorize entities such as people, organizations, and locations in text, helping analysts quickly extract relevant information from large volumes of unstructured data.

Example:

NLP tools could analyze tweets and news articles related to a geopolitical conflict to identify key figures, organizations, and sentiment shifts, providing valuable insights into the situation.

3. Multimodal AI Systems

Overview:

Multimodal AI systems integrate and analyze data from multiple sources and modalities, such as text, images, audio, and video. This holistic approach allows for a more comprehensive understanding of the data, enabling more accurate and nuanced intelligence.

Applications in OSINT:

- **Integrated Analysis**: Combining text analysis with image and video recognition can provide a fuller picture of online activities and threats. For instance, a multimodal system could correlate a suspicious social media post with images or videos related to the same topic.
- **Enhanced Search Capabilities**: Multimodal AI can improve search functions by allowing users to query using various types of data, such as searching for specific objects in images or patterns in audio recordings.

Example:

A multimodal AI system could analyze video footage from a public protest and cross-reference it with social media posts to identify key participants and understand the context of the event.

4. AI-Powered Cyber Threat Intelligence Platforms

Overview:

AI-powered threat intelligence platforms use machine learning and data analytics to aggregate, analyze, and contextualize threat data from various sources. These platforms can provide actionable insights and predictions about potential cyber threats.

Applications in OSINT:

- **Threat Aggregation**: AI platforms can gather threat data from diverse sources, including dark web forums, social media, and technical blogs, to create a comprehensive threat landscape.
- **Predictive Analytics**: By analyzing historical threat data and current trends, AI can predict future threats and provide early warnings to organizations.

Example:

An AI-powered threat intelligence platform might analyze data from multiple sources to identify a new ransomware strain and predict its potential targets based on emerging patterns.

5. Autonomous Data Collection Agents

Overview:

Autonomous data collection agents are AI-driven tools that can independently gather data from various sources without human intervention. These agents use web crawlers, API integrations, and other methods to continuously collect and update information.

Applications in OSINT:

- **Continuous Monitoring**: Autonomous agents can monitor online sources 24/7, ensuring that intelligence is always up-to-date and relevant.
- **Dynamic Data Collection**: These agents can adapt their data collection strategies based on evolving requirements or emerging threats.

Example:

An autonomous data collection agent might continuously scrape dark web forums for information related to specific cybersecurity threats, updating threat intelligence databases in real-time.

6. Explainable AI (XAI) for Transparency

Overview:

Explainable AI (XAI) focuses on making AI models and their decisions more transparent and understandable to humans. This is crucial for ensuring that AI systems are used ethically and that their outputs can be trusted.

Applications in OSINT:

- **Decision Transparency**: XAI can provide insights into how AI models arrive at their conclusions, helping analysts understand the rationale behind threat assessments and predictions.
- **Bias Detection**: By explaining AI decision-making processes, XAI can help identify and address biases in models, ensuring fair and accurate intelligence.

Example:

An XAI system might explain why a particular social media post was flagged as suspicious, providing details on the factors considered and helping analysts validate the result.

7. AI-Driven Network Analysis Tools

Overview:

AI-driven network analysis tools use machine learning algorithms to analyze and visualize complex networks, such as social networks, communication networks, and cyberattack networks. These tools can reveal hidden relationships and patterns within the data.

Applications in OSINT:

- **Relationship Mapping**: AI can map relationships between entities, such as individuals, organizations, or IP addresses, to uncover connections that may indicate a coordinated threat.
- **Network Visualization**: Advanced visualization techniques can help analysts understand the structure and dynamics of complex networks, facilitating more effective threat analysis.

Example:

An AI-driven network analysis tool might visualize connections between different cybercriminal groups based on communication patterns, revealing potential collaboration or shared tactics.

8. Context-Aware AI Systems

Overview:

Context-aware AI systems are designed to understand and consider the context in which data is generated and analyzed. This includes temporal, spatial, and situational contexts that can significantly impact the interpretation of information.

Applications in OSINT:

- **Contextual Analysis**: AI systems can analyze data within its specific context, such as the geographical location of a threat or the timing of an event, to provide more accurate and relevant insights.
- **Adaptive Responses**: Context-aware systems can adapt their analysis and recommendations based on the current situation or changes in the environment.

Example:

A context-aware AI system might assess a potential security threat based on the current geopolitical climate and recent events, providing tailored intelligence relevant to the situation.

9. Blockchain for Secure Data Sharing

Overview:

Blockchain technology offers a decentralized and secure way to record and share data. AI can leverage blockchain to enhance the security and integrity of OSINT data.

Applications in OSINT:

- **Data Integrity**: Blockchain can ensure the integrity of OSINT data by providing a tamper-proof record of data collection and analysis.
- **Secure Sharing**: Blockchain enables secure and transparent sharing of intelligence data between organizations, reducing the risk of data tampering or unauthorized access.

Example:

A blockchain-based system might record and validate threat intelligence data from multiple sources, ensuring that all parties have access to accurate and unaltered information.

10. AI-Enhanced Personalization

Overview:

AI-enhanced personalization involves tailoring intelligence outputs and recommendations based on individual user preferences and needs. This can improve the relevance and utility of OSINT for different users and organizations.

Applications in OSINT:

- **Customized Intelligence**: AI can provide personalized intelligence reports and alerts based on specific user interests, roles, and requirements.
- **User-Centric Design**: AI systems can adapt their interfaces and functionalities to better meet the needs of individual users, improving overall effectiveness.

Example:

An AI system might generate customized threat intelligence reports for different departments within an organization, focusing on the specific types of threats relevant to each department's functions.

Emerging AI technologies are set to revolutionize the field of OSINT by providing new capabilities for data collection, analysis, and threat detection. From generative models and advanced NLP to multimodal systems and autonomous agents, these innovations will enhance the effectiveness and efficiency of intelligence operations. As these technologies continue to develop, they will offer increasingly sophisticated tools for understanding and mitigating cyber threats, shaping the future of AI-driven OSINT.

10.2. The Impact of AI on Future Cyber Threats

The rapid advancement of Artificial Intelligence (AI) is reshaping the landscape of cybersecurity, bringing both opportunities and challenges. As AI technologies become more sophisticated, they are likely to have a profound impact on the nature of cyber threats and the strategies used to combat them. This section explores how AI is expected to influence future cyber threats, examining both the potential risks and the ways in which AI can be harnessed to strengthen cybersecurity defenses.

1. Evolution of Sophisticated Attack Techniques

Overview:

AI's capabilities to analyze and generate data can be exploited by cybercriminals to develop more sophisticated and targeted attack techniques. Machine learning algorithms can be used to create advanced malware, craft highly personalized phishing attacks, and automate various aspects of cybercrime.

Implications:

- **Advanced Malware**: AI can be used to develop malware that adapts to different environments, evades detection by traditional security tools, and even learns from interactions with security systems.
- **Personalized Phishing**: AI can analyze vast amounts of personal data to craft highly targeted phishing attacks that are more likely to deceive victims. This personalization increases the effectiveness of social engineering attacks.
- **Automated Attacks**: AI-driven automation allows cybercriminals to execute large-scale attacks with precision and efficiency, targeting multiple vulnerabilities simultaneously.

Example:

An AI-powered ransomware could dynamically adjust its encryption methods and attack vectors based on the defenses it encounters, making it harder for security systems to detect and neutralize the threat.

2. Increased Threat of AI-Powered Cyber Espionage

Overview:

AI can be utilized for cyber espionage, enabling adversaries to conduct more effective and covert surveillance. By leveraging AI for data analysis and pattern recognition, cyber spies can gather and exploit sensitive information more efficiently.

Implications:

- **Enhanced Data Collection**: AI tools can automate the collection and analysis of large volumes of data from various sources, including social media, communications, and dark web forums.
- **Improved Targeting**: AI can identify high-value targets and vulnerabilities with greater accuracy, leading to more successful espionage operations.
- **Stealthier Operations**: AI can help adversaries conduct surveillance and infiltration activities without detection, using techniques such as automated keylogging and behavioral analysis.

Example:

An AI system might analyze communication patterns within a government agency to identify key personnel and sensitive information, leading to more effective espionage efforts and potential data breaches.

3. Emergence of Autonomous Cyber Attacks

Overview:

The development of autonomous AI systems could lead to the emergence of self-directed cyber attacks. These systems could operate independently, making decisions and executing attacks based on their programmed objectives.

Implications:

- **Self-Learning Attacks**: Autonomous AI systems could learn from their environment and adapt their strategies in real-time, increasing the complexity and unpredictability of attacks.
- **Scalable Attacks:** AI-powered autonomous systems can scale their operations to target multiple systems or organizations simultaneously, amplifying the impact of cyber attacks.
- **Minimal Human Intervention**: Cyber attacks could be carried out with little to no human oversight, making it challenging for defenders to anticipate and counteract the threats.

Example:

An autonomous AI-driven attack system might autonomously identify and exploit vulnerabilities across a network, executing coordinated attacks on various targets without human intervention.

4. Exploitation of AI Vulnerabilities

Overview:

As AI technologies become more integrated into cybersecurity systems, they also introduce new vulnerabilities. Attackers may seek to exploit weaknesses in AI models, data sources, and algorithms to undermine security measures.

Implications:

- **Adversarial Attacks**: Attackers can use adversarial techniques to manipulate AI models, causing them to make incorrect predictions or classifications. This could lead to security systems failing to detect threats or responding inappropriately.
- **Data Poisoning**: Malicious actors might poison training data used by AI systems, leading to biased or flawed models that reduce the effectiveness of security measures.
- **Model Theft**: AI models themselves could be targeted for theft or reverse engineering, allowing attackers to understand and potentially exploit their weaknesses.

Example:

An attacker might conduct a data poisoning attack on an AI-based intrusion detection system, introducing malicious data to corrupt the model and reduce its ability to detect real threats.

5. Enhanced Privacy Risks and Surveillance

Overview:

The use of AI in cyber threats also raises significant privacy concerns. AI-driven surveillance and data collection can lead to increased risks of privacy invasion and unauthorized access to personal information.

Implications:

- **Mass Surveillance**: AI technologies can enable extensive surveillance operations, tracking individuals' online activities and communications on a large scale.
- **Data Breaches**: The aggregation of personal data by AI systems increases the risk of large-scale data breaches, with potentially severe consequences for affected individuals.
- **Ethical Concerns**: The deployment of AI for surveillance raises ethical questions about consent, transparency, and the balance between security and privacy.

Example:

An AI-driven surveillance system might analyze data from social media and communications to track and profile individuals, raising concerns about privacy violations and unauthorized data access.

6. AI-Enhanced Threat Intelligence and Countermeasures

Overview:

On a positive note, AI can also be used to enhance threat intelligence and cybersecurity defenses. By leveraging AI for threat detection, analysis, and response, organizations can improve their ability to combat emerging threats.

Implications:

- **Advanced Detection**: AI systems can analyze vast amounts of data to detect patterns and anomalies indicative of cyber threats, providing early warnings and improving response times.
- **Automated Response**: AI can automate incident response processes, such as isolating compromised systems or applying security patches, to reduce the impact of attacks.
- **Predictive Analytics**: AI can use predictive analytics to anticipate future threats and recommend proactive measures to mitigate potential risks.

Example:

An AI-powered threat intelligence platform might aggregate and analyze data from multiple sources to identify new and emerging threats, providing actionable insights and recommendations to enhance cybersecurity defenses.

7. Collaboration and Intelligence Sharing

Overview:

AI has the potential to facilitate collaboration and intelligence sharing between organizations and government agencies. By improving the exchange of threat information and best practices, AI can enhance collective cybersecurity efforts.

Implications:

- **Enhanced Collaboration**: AI tools can facilitate the sharing of threat intelligence and best practices between organizations, improving the collective defense against cyber threats.

- **Integrated Defense Systems**: AI can enable the integration of security measures across different organizations and sectors, creating a more cohesive and effective defense strategy.
- **Cross-Organizational Insights**: AI can provide insights into trends and patterns across multiple organizations, helping to identify and address common threats.

Example:

AI-driven platforms might enable real-time sharing of threat data between financial institutions and government agencies, improving the ability to detect and respond to financial fraud and cybercrime.

The impact of AI on future cyber threats is multifaceted, with both potential risks and opportunities. While AI can enable more sophisticated and autonomous attacks, it also offers powerful tools for enhancing cybersecurity defenses and threat intelligence. As AI technologies continue to evolve, it is crucial for organizations to stay informed about emerging threats and leverage AI to strengthen their security measures. By understanding and addressing the potential impacts of AI on cyber threats, organizations can better prepare for and defend against the challenges of the future.

10.3. The Evolution of OSINT Methodologies

Open Source Intelligence (OSINT) has significantly evolved from its early beginnings to become a critical component of modern intelligence and cybersecurity operations. This evolution reflects changes in technology, data availability, and analytical techniques. This section explores the progression of OSINT methodologies, highlighting key developments and how they have transformed the field.

1. Early OSINT Techniques

Overview:

In its early stages, OSINT primarily involved manual collection and analysis of publicly available information. This included traditional methods such as reviewing print media, public records, and other tangible sources.

Key Characteristics:

- **Manual Research**: Analysts manually searched newspapers, magazines, government reports, and other physical sources for relevant information.
- **Limited Scope**: Data collection was constrained by the availability and accessibility of physical sources, which limited the volume and diversity of information that could be gathered.
- **Basic Analysis**: Analysis involved straightforward techniques such as summarizing reports and identifying key facts without the aid of advanced tools or technologies.

Example:

In the pre-digital era, intelligence agencies might have relied on newspaper archives and public records to gather information on geopolitical developments or emerging threats.

2. The Advent of Digital OSINT

Overview:

The rise of digital technologies in the late 20th and early 21st centuries marked a significant shift in OSINT methodologies. The internet, online databases, and digital communication channels provided new opportunities for data collection and analysis.

Key Characteristics:

- **Digital Databases**: Analysts began using online databases, such as news archives and academic journals, to access a broader range of information quickly.
- **Search Engines**: The development of search engines revolutionized data retrieval, enabling analysts to find relevant information more efficiently.
- **Email and Forums**: The proliferation of email and online forums introduced new sources of information, including user-generated content and discussions.

Example:

With the advent of search engines like Google, OSINT analysts could quickly locate and gather information from a vast array of online sources, including news articles, research papers, and social media discussions.

3. Social Media and Web 2.0 Era

Overview:

The emergence of social media platforms and Web 2.0 technologies in the 2000s further transformed OSINT methodologies. Social media provided real-time access to user-generated content and insights into public sentiment.

Key Characteristics:

- **Real-Time Data**: Social media platforms like Twitter, Facebook, and LinkedIn offered real-time updates on events, trends, and individual activities.
- **User-Generated Content**: Analysts gained access to a wealth of user-generated content, including posts, photos, and videos, which provided valuable insights into various topics.
- **Social Network Analysis**: The ability to analyze social networks and connections enabled the identification of influential individuals, groups, and emerging trends.

Example:

During significant global events, such as protests or natural disasters, social media platforms became critical sources of real-time information, allowing analysts to monitor developments and assess public reactions.

4. Advanced Data Analytics and Big Data

Overview:

The development of advanced data analytics and big data technologies in the 2010s enhanced OSINT methodologies by enabling the analysis of large volumes of data from diverse sources.

Key Characteristics:

- **Big Data Tools**: The use of big data tools and technologies allowed for the aggregation, storage, and analysis of massive datasets, including structured and unstructured data.
- **Data Mining**: Data mining techniques were employed to uncover patterns, trends, and correlations within large datasets, providing deeper insights into complex issues.

- **Visualization**: Advanced visualization tools enabled analysts to present data in meaningful ways, such as through interactive dashboards and graphical representations.

Example:

Big data analytics platforms could analyze vast amounts of social media data to identify emerging trends, monitor public sentiment, and detect potential threats or issues before they escalate.

5. Integration of AI and Machine Learning

Overview:

The integration of Artificial Intelligence (AI) and machine learning into OSINT methodologies represents a significant advancement. AI technologies enhance the capabilities of data collection, analysis, and interpretation.

Key Characteristics:

- **Automated Data Collection**: AI-driven tools automate the collection of data from various sources, including websites, social media, and databases, reducing manual effort and increasing efficiency.
- **Natural Language Processing (NLP)**: NLP techniques enable the analysis of text data, including sentiment analysis, entity recognition, and topic modeling, to extract valuable insights.
- **Pattern Recognition**: Machine learning algorithms can identify patterns and anomalies in data, improving threat detection and predictive analytics.

Example:

AI-powered tools might analyze social media posts to detect early signs of coordinated disinformation campaigns or identify emerging cyber threats based on patterns in online behavior.

6. Integration of Geospatial Intelligence (GEOINT)

Overview:

The integration of geospatial intelligence (GEOINT) with OSINT methodologies adds a spatial dimension to data analysis, enhancing the ability to visualize and interpret information based on geographical context.

Key Characteristics:

- **Geospatial Data Analysis**: GEOINT tools analyze spatial data, such as satellite imagery and geographic information systems (GIS), to provide context and insights into various phenomena.
- **Location-Based Insights**: Integrating geospatial data with OSINT allows for the identification of location-specific trends, patterns, and threats.
- **Mapping and Visualization**: Advanced mapping and visualization techniques help analysts understand and communicate spatial relationships and patterns.

Example:

Combining social media data with geospatial analysis might reveal the geographical spread of a protest or the location of key infrastructure that could be targeted in a cyberattack.

7. The Future of OSINT Methodologies

Overview:

Looking ahead, OSINT methodologies are expected to continue evolving with advancements in technology, data sources, and analytical techniques. Emerging trends include greater integration of AI, increased automation, and more sophisticated data visualization tools.

Key Characteristics:

- **Enhanced Automation**: Future OSINT methodologies will likely see increased automation in data collection and analysis, enabling more efficient and scalable intelligence operations.
- **AI Integration**: AI will continue to play a central role in enhancing OSINT capabilities, providing advanced tools for data analysis, threat detection, and predictive analytics.
- **Ethical Considerations**: As OSINT methodologies become more advanced, there will be a growing emphasis on addressing ethical and privacy concerns, ensuring responsible and transparent use of intelligence tools.

Example:

Future OSINT platforms might combine real-time data from a wide range of sources with advanced AI-driven analytics to provide actionable insights and early warnings for a variety of threats and opportunities.

The evolution of OSINT methodologies reflects the dynamic nature of technology and data. From early manual techniques to advanced AI-driven tools, each phase of development has expanded the capabilities of OSINT and enhanced its role in intelligence and cybersecurity. As technology continues to advance, OSINT methodologies will likely continue to evolve, offering new opportunities and challenges for analysts and decision-makers. Understanding this evolution is crucial for leveraging OSINT effectively and staying ahead in the rapidly changing landscape of intelligence and security.

10.4. Preparing for AI-Driven Intelligence Gathering

As Artificial Intelligence (AI) increasingly becomes a core component of intelligence gathering and analysis, organizations must adapt to harness its full potential while addressing associated challenges. Preparing for AI-driven intelligence gathering involves understanding the technology, implementing strategic changes, and developing best practices to ensure effective and ethical use. This section outlines key considerations and steps for preparing for AI-driven intelligence gathering.

1. Understanding AI Capabilities and Limitations

Overview:

- Before integrating AI into intelligence gathering processes, it's crucial to have a clear understanding of its capabilities and limitations. AI technologies offer advanced data analysis, pattern recognition, and automation, but they also come with constraints that must be managed.

Key Considerations:

- **Capabilities**: AI can process and analyze large volumes of data quickly, identify complex patterns, and provide predictive insights. This enables more efficient and accurate intelligence gathering.

- **Limitations**: AI systems are not infallible. They depend on the quality of input data and may struggle with ambiguous or incomplete information. Understanding these limitations helps in setting realistic expectations and avoiding overreliance on AI.

Example:

AI-driven systems can rapidly analyze social media data to identify trends and potential threats. However, they may require human oversight to interpret nuanced context and verify findings.

2. Selecting the Right AI Tools and Platforms

Overview:

Choosing the appropriate AI tools and platforms is critical for effective intelligence gathering. Different tools offer various functionalities, such as data collection, analysis, visualization, and integration.

Key Considerations:

- **Tool Functionality**: Assess the specific functionalities of AI tools, including their capabilities in data collection, processing, and analysis. Ensure that the tools align with your organization's intelligence needs.
- **Integration**: Evaluate how well AI tools integrate with existing systems and workflows. Seamless integration ensures that AI enhances rather than disrupts current processes.
- **Scalability**: Choose tools that can scale with your organization's needs, accommodating increasing data volumes and evolving requirements.

Example:

An organization might select an AI platform that specializes in natural language processing (NLP) for analyzing large volumes of textual data from various sources, integrating it with existing data management systems.

3. Developing Data Management Strategies

Overview:

Effective data management is essential for leveraging AI in intelligence gathering. AI systems rely on high-quality, relevant data to deliver accurate insights.

Key Considerations:

- **Data Quality**: Implement processes to ensure data accuracy, completeness, and relevance. AI systems perform best with clean, well-organized data.
- **Data Integration**: Develop strategies for integrating data from diverse sources, such as social media, public records, and proprietary databases. Unified data sources enhance the effectiveness of AI analysis.
- **Data Privacy and Security**: Ensure that data management practices comply with privacy regulations and security standards. Protect sensitive information and maintain data integrity.

Example:

A data management strategy might involve regular data cleansing, establishing data governance policies, and employing encryption techniques to safeguard sensitive information used by AI systems.

4. Training and Skill Development

Overview:

To effectively use AI in intelligence gathering, organizations must invest in training and skill development. Ensuring that staff have the necessary expertise is critical for maximizing AI's benefits.

Key Considerations:

- **Training Programs**: Develop training programs for staff to familiarize them with AI tools, methodologies, and best practices. Training should cover both technical aspects and practical applications.
- **Skill Development**: Encourage ongoing skill development to keep pace with advances in AI technology. This includes staying informed about new tools, techniques, and trends in AI and intelligence gathering.
- **Collaboration**: Foster collaboration between data scientists, intelligence analysts, and other relevant stakeholders to ensure effective use of AI and integration with existing workflows.

Example:

Conducting workshops and training sessions on AI tools and techniques can help intelligence analysts understand how to leverage AI for data analysis, threat detection, and decision-making.

5. Implementing Ethical Guidelines and Best Practices

Overview:

Ethical considerations are paramount when using AI for intelligence gathering. Implementing guidelines and best practices ensures responsible and transparent use of AI technologies.

Key Considerations:

- **Ethical Guidelines**: Establish ethical guidelines to govern the use of AI in intelligence gathering. This includes considerations related to privacy, bias, and transparency.
- **Bias Mitigation**: Develop strategies to identify and mitigate biases in AI algorithms. Ensuring fairness and objectivity in AI-driven analysis is essential for credible intelligence.
- **Transparency and Accountability**: Promote transparency in AI operations and decision-making processes. Ensure that there are mechanisms for accountability and oversight.

Example:

Implementing regular audits of AI systems to check for biases and ensuring that AI-generated insights are reviewed by human experts can help maintain ethical standards in intelligence gathering.

6. Preparing for Change Management

Overview:

Integrating AI into intelligence gathering may require significant changes to existing processes and workflows. Effective change management is crucial for smooth implementation and adoption.

Key Considerations:

- **Change Management Plan**: Develop a change management plan to address potential challenges and resistance. This plan should outline steps for integrating AI, including communication, training, and support.
- **Stakeholder Engagement**: Engage stakeholders throughout the implementation process to ensure their needs and concerns are addressed. Collaboration with key personnel helps facilitate a smoother transition.
- **Monitoring and Evaluation**: Continuously monitor and evaluate the impact of AI integration on intelligence gathering processes. Adjust strategies as needed to optimize performance and address any issues.

Example:

A change management plan might include regular updates to staff on the progress of AI integration, providing support resources, and soliciting feedback to address any concerns or challenges.

7. Establishing Performance Metrics and Evaluation

Overview:

To assess the effectiveness of AI-driven intelligence gathering, organizations must establish performance metrics and evaluation criteria. This helps measure the impact of AI and identify areas for improvement.

Key Considerations:

- **Performance Metrics**: Define clear metrics to evaluate the performance of AI tools and systems. Metrics may include accuracy, efficiency, and the relevance of insights generated.
- **Evaluation Processes**: Implement processes for regularly evaluating AI performance and effectiveness. This includes reviewing outcomes, analyzing feedback, and making necessary adjustments.
- **Continuous Improvement**: Use evaluation results to drive continuous improvement in AI-driven intelligence gathering. Adjust tools, processes, and strategies based on performance insights.

Example:

Metrics such as the accuracy of threat detection, the speed of data processing, and user satisfaction can be used to evaluate the effectiveness of AI tools and identify areas for enhancement.

Preparing for AI-driven intelligence gathering involves understanding AI capabilities, selecting appropriate tools, managing data effectively, training staff, implementing ethical guidelines, and managing change. By addressing these areas, organizations can harness the full potential of AI while ensuring responsible and effective use. As AI continues to evolve, ongoing adaptation and preparation will be key to maintaining a competitive edge and achieving successful intelligence outcomes.

10.5. The Next Frontier: AI in Autonomous Investigations

As AI technology continues to advance, the concept of autonomous investigations is emerging as a significant frontier in the field of intelligence and cybersecurity. Autonomous investigations involve leveraging AI systems to independently conduct and complete investigative tasks with minimal human intervention. This section explores the potential of AI in autonomous investigations, the technology behind it, its benefits, challenges, and future prospects.

1. Defining Autonomous Investigations

Overview:

Autonomous investigations refer to the use of AI technologies to perform investigative tasks independently, without the need for continuous human oversight. These tasks can range from data collection and analysis to decision-making and reporting.

Key Characteristics:

- **Self-Sufficiency**: Autonomous systems operate with a high degree of self-sufficiency, capable of executing complex tasks and making decisions based on predefined rules and learned patterns.
- **Automation**: These systems automate repetitive and data-intensive tasks, reducing the need for manual intervention and allowing human investigators to focus on higher-level strategic activities.
- **Learning and Adaptation**: Advanced AI systems can learn from new data and adapt their methods over time, improving their performance and accuracy.

Example:

An autonomous investigation system might monitor network traffic for unusual patterns, analyze them to identify potential security threats, and generate detailed reports on its findings with minimal human involvement.

2. Technologies Driving Autonomous Investigations

Overview:

Several key AI technologies are driving the development of autonomous investigations. These technologies enable systems to operate independently and perform investigative tasks with high efficiency.

Key Technologies:

- **Machine Learning (ML):** ML algorithms enable systems to learn from data and make predictions or decisions based on patterns and trends. This includes supervised, unsupervised, and reinforcement learning techniques.
- **Natural Language Processing (NLP):** NLP allows systems to understand, interpret, and generate human language, enabling them to process and analyze textual data from various sources.
- **Robotic Process Automation (RPA):** RPA involves automating repetitive tasks through software robots, such as data extraction and report generation, which can be integrated into autonomous investigation systems.
- **AI-Based Decision Making**: AI systems use decision-making algorithms to evaluate data and make informed decisions or recommendations, often based on complex criteria and learned experiences.

Example:

An autonomous investigation system might use NLP to analyze social media posts for signs of coordinated disinformation campaigns and then apply ML algorithms to assess the potential impact and generate responses.

3. Benefits of Autonomous Investigations

Overview:

The adoption of autonomous investigations offers numerous benefits, enhancing efficiency, accuracy, and scalability in investigative processes.

Key Benefits:

- **Increased Efficiency**: Autonomous systems can process and analyze large volumes of data at high speed, significantly improving the efficiency of investigations.
- **Enhanced Accuracy**: By minimizing human error and leveraging advanced algorithms, autonomous systems can provide more accurate and reliable insights.
- **Scalability**: These systems can handle vast amounts of data and numerous investigations simultaneously, making them highly scalable and adaptable to various needs.
- **Cost Savings**: Reducing the need for manual labor and streamlining processes can lead to cost savings for organizations, allowing resources to be allocated more effectively.

Example:

A financial institution might use an autonomous investigation system to continuously monitor transactions for signs of fraudulent activity, allowing for real-time detection and response while reducing the need for manual review.

4. Challenges and Considerations

Overview:

Despite the advantages, autonomous investigations come with several challenges and considerations that organizations must address to ensure effective and responsible use.

Key Challenges:

- **Algorithmic Bias**: AI systems can inadvertently perpetuate biases present in the training data, leading to skewed results and potentially unfair outcomes. Addressing bias requires careful data management and algorithm design.
- **Ethical and Privacy Concerns**: Autonomous investigations may raise ethical and privacy issues, such as the handling of sensitive data and the potential for invasive monitoring. Implementing strict guidelines and ensuring transparency are essential.

- **Complexity of Integration**: Integrating autonomous systems into existing workflows and infrastructure can be complex, requiring careful planning and coordination to ensure seamless operation.
- **Dependence on Data Quality**: The performance of autonomous systems heavily relies on the quality of the data they process. Poor-quality or incomplete data can impact the accuracy and effectiveness of investigations.

Example:

An autonomous investigation system used for monitoring employee communications might inadvertently produce biased results if the algorithms used are not properly vetted for fairness and accuracy.

5. Future Prospects and Developments

Overview:

The future of autonomous investigations holds exciting prospects as AI technology continues to evolve. Advancements in AI, data analytics, and automation are likely to further enhance the capabilities and applications of autonomous systems.

Key Trends:

- **Advanced AI Models**: Future developments in AI models, including more sophisticated neural networks and hybrid approaches, will enhance the capabilities of autonomous systems.
- **Greater Integration**: Autonomous investigation systems will increasingly integrate with other technologies, such as the Internet of Things (IoT) and blockchain, to provide more comprehensive and interconnected solutions.
- **Enhanced Human-AI Collaboration**: While autonomous systems will take on more tasks independently, there will be a growing emphasis on collaboration between humans and AI, combining the strengths of both for optimal results.
- **Regulation and Oversight**: As autonomous investigations become more prevalent, regulatory frameworks and oversight mechanisms will be developed to ensure ethical and responsible use of these technologies.

Example:

In the future, autonomous investigation systems might incorporate advanced AI models capable of understanding and responding to complex, context-specific scenarios, such as detecting emerging threats in dynamic environments.

6. Preparing for Autonomous Investigations

Overview:

Organizations looking to adopt autonomous investigations should prepare by addressing key aspects such as technology selection, ethical considerations, and integration strategies.

Key Preparations:

- **Technology Assessment**: Evaluate and select AI technologies that align with your organization's needs and capabilities. Consider factors such as scalability, integration, and support.
- **Ethical Guidelines**: Develop ethical guidelines and policies to govern the use of autonomous systems, ensuring that they adhere to privacy, fairness, and transparency standards.
- **Training and Support**: Provide training for staff to understand and effectively use autonomous systems. Establish support mechanisms to address technical issues and ensure smooth operation.
- **Continuous Evaluation**: Implement processes for continuously evaluating the performance and impact of autonomous systems, making adjustments as needed to improve effectiveness and address any challenges.

Example:

An organization implementing an autonomous investigation system for cybersecurity might develop a comprehensive training program for its IT staff, establish ethical guidelines for data use, and regularly review system performance to ensure alignment with organizational goals.

The advent of AI-driven autonomous investigations represents a significant advancement in intelligence and cybersecurity. By leveraging autonomous systems, organizations can enhance their investigative capabilities, improve efficiency, and gain deeper insights. However, addressing challenges such as algorithmic bias, ethical concerns, and integration complexity is essential for successful implementation. As technology continues to evolve, autonomous investigations will play an increasingly important role in shaping the future of intelligence and security. Preparing for this next frontier involves careful planning, strategic implementation, and ongoing evaluation to maximize the benefits and ensure responsible use of AI technologies.

Chapter 11: Practical Implementation and Challenges

Chapter 11, "Practical Implementation and Challenges," offers a hands-on guide to integrating Artificial Intelligence (AI) into Open Source Intelligence (OSINT) workflows. This chapter provides practical advice on how to implement AI-driven solutions effectively, from initial setup and customization to scaling and optimizing their use. It addresses common challenges encountered during implementation, such as technical difficulties, integration with existing systems, and managing change within an organization. By providing strategies for overcoming these obstacles and best practices for successful AI adoption, this chapter aims to equip professionals with the knowledge needed to harness the full potential of AI in their OSINT operations.

11.1. Steps to Integrate AI into OSINT Workflows

Integrating Artificial Intelligence (AI) into Open Source Intelligence (OSINT) workflows involves a systematic approach to enhance the efficiency and effectiveness of intelligence gathering and analysis. This integration requires careful planning, technology selection, and process adjustments to ensure that AI tools complement and enhance existing OSINT practices. This section outlines key steps to successfully integrate AI into OSINT workflows.

1. Assess Organizational Needs and Objectives

Overview:

Before integrating AI, it is essential to assess your organization's needs and objectives to ensure that the chosen AI solutions align with your OSINT goals.

Steps:

- **Identify Objectives**: Define the specific objectives you aim to achieve with AI integration, such as improving data analysis, automating repetitive tasks, or enhancing threat detection capabilities.
- **Evaluate Current Workflows**: Analyze existing OSINT workflows to identify areas where AI can provide the most value. This includes examining data collection methods, analysis processes, and reporting systems.

- **Set Clear Goals**: Establish clear, measurable goals for AI integration, such as reducing the time required for data analysis or increasing the accuracy of threat identification.

Example:

An organization might identify the need to streamline the process of analyzing large volumes of social media data to detect emerging threats more efficiently.

2. Select Appropriate AI Tools and Technologies

Overview:

Choosing the right AI tools and technologies is crucial for effective integration. Different tools offer various functionalities, and selecting those that best fit your needs is essential.

Steps:

- **Research Available Tools**: Explore AI tools and platforms that specialize in areas relevant to your OSINT objectives, such as natural language processing (NLP), machine learning (ML), or image recognition.
- **Evaluate Features**: Assess the features and capabilities of different AI tools, including their ability to handle specific types of data, integration capabilities, and ease of use.
- **Consider Scalability**: Choose tools that can scale with your organization's needs, accommodating increasing data volumes and evolving requirements.

Example:

Selecting an NLP tool that can analyze and categorize textual data from various sources, combined with a machine learning platform for pattern recognition, may be appropriate for enhancing OSINT analysis.

3. Develop an Integration Strategy

Overview:

An effective integration strategy outlines how AI tools will be incorporated into existing OSINT workflows, ensuring a smooth transition and minimizing disruption.

Steps:

- **Create a Plan**: Develop a detailed plan for integrating AI into your workflows, including timelines, resource allocation, and key milestones.
- **Define Integration Points**: Identify where AI tools will fit into current processes, such as data collection, analysis, or reporting. Determine how they will interact with existing systems.
- **Ensure Compatibility**: Ensure that AI tools are compatible with your current infrastructure and can integrate with other systems used in your OSINT operations.

Example:

A plan might involve integrating an AI-based data collection tool into your existing OSINT platform, allowing for seamless data aggregation and analysis.

4. Train and Support Personnel

Overview:

Training and supporting personnel is essential for the successful adoption of AI tools. Staff need to understand how to use these tools effectively and adapt to new workflows.

Steps:

- **Conduct Training**: Provide comprehensive training for staff on how to use AI tools and incorporate them into their daily tasks. Training should cover both technical aspects and practical applications.
- **Offer Ongoing Support**: Establish support mechanisms to assist personnel with any issues or questions that arise during the transition. This may include help desks, user guides, and technical support.
- **Encourage Collaboration**: Foster collaboration between data scientists, OSINT analysts, and other relevant stakeholders to facilitate knowledge sharing and problem-solving.

Example:

Training sessions on the use of AI-based analytics tools might be conducted for OSINT analysts, with additional resources available for troubleshooting and advanced support.

5. Implement AI Tools and Monitor Performance

Overview:

Once AI tools are integrated, it is important to implement them effectively and continuously monitor their performance to ensure they meet the desired objectives.

Steps:

- **Deploy Tools**: Roll out AI tools according to the integration plan, ensuring that they are properly configured and operational.
- **Monitor Performance**: Regularly monitor the performance of AI tools to assess their effectiveness and identify any issues. Use performance metrics to evaluate their impact on OSINT workflows.
- **Collect Feedback**: Gather feedback from users to understand their experiences with the AI tools and identify areas for improvement.

Example:

Monitoring might involve tracking the accuracy of threat detection by AI tools and comparing it to previous methods, as well as collecting user feedback on ease of use and functionality.

6. Optimize and Refine Workflows

Overview:

Based on performance monitoring and feedback, optimize and refine your OSINT workflows to maximize the benefits of AI integration.

Steps:

- **Analyze Results**: Review the results of performance monitoring and user feedback to identify areas where AI tools can be improved or adjusted.
- **Make Adjustments**: Implement changes to optimize workflows, such as refining AI algorithms, adjusting integration points, or enhancing data processing methods.

- **Continuously Improve**: Adopt a continuous improvement approach, regularly updating and refining AI tools and workflows to adapt to new challenges and opportunities.

Example:

If feedback indicates that an AI tool is producing false positives in threat detection, adjustments to the algorithm or additional training data might be necessary to improve accuracy.

7. Address Ethical and Compliance Considerations

Overview:

Integrating AI into OSINT workflows involves addressing ethical and compliance considerations to ensure responsible and lawful use of technology.

Steps:

- **Establish Guidelines**: Develop ethical guidelines for the use of AI in OSINT, covering issues such as data privacy, bias, and transparency.
- **Ensure Compliance**: Ensure that AI tools and processes comply with relevant regulations and standards, such as data protection laws and industry best practices.
- **Conduct Audits**: Regularly audit AI systems and workflows to ensure adherence to ethical guidelines and legal requirements.

Example:

Implementing a policy for regular audits of AI-generated data to ensure compliance with data protection regulations and address any ethical concerns related to data use.

8. Scale and Adapt AI Integration

Overview:

As your organization's needs evolve, scaling and adapting AI integration becomes important to maintain effectiveness and address new challenges.

Steps:

- **Plan for Scaling**: Develop a strategy for scaling AI tools and processes to accommodate growing data volumes and expanding needs. This may involve upgrading infrastructure or adding new tools.
- **Adapt to Changes**: Stay informed about advancements in AI technology and adapt your integration strategy accordingly. This includes incorporating new features, tools, or methodologies as they become available.
- **Evaluate Impact**: Continuously evaluate the impact of scaled and adapted AI integration on OSINT workflows, ensuring that it continues to meet organizational objectives.

Example:

As your organization's data sources expand, you might need to integrate additional AI tools or upgrade existing ones to handle increased data volumes and maintain effective analysis.

Integrating AI into OSINT workflows requires a structured approach, including assessing needs, selecting appropriate tools, developing integration strategies, and providing training and support. Monitoring performance, optimizing workflows, addressing ethical considerations, and planning for scalability are also crucial for successful integration. By following these steps, organizations can effectively leverage AI to enhance their OSINT capabilities, improve efficiency, and achieve better intelligence outcomes.

11.2. Overcoming Technical Challenges in AI-OSINT Integration

Integrating Artificial Intelligence (AI) into Open Source Intelligence (OSINT) workflows presents a range of technical challenges that can impact the effectiveness and efficiency of the integration process. Addressing these challenges is crucial for ensuring that AI tools enhance rather than hinder OSINT capabilities. This section explores common technical challenges in AI-OSINT integration and provides strategies for overcoming them.

1. Data Quality and Integration

Overview:

High-quality data is essential for the effective functioning of AI systems. However, integrating AI into OSINT workflows often involves dealing with diverse and unstructured data sources, which can affect the quality and consistency of the data used for analysis.

Challenges:

- **Data Variability**: OSINT involves collecting data from various sources, including social media, websites, and databases, which can vary significantly in format and quality.
- **Data Preprocessing**: Raw data often requires preprocessing to clean and standardize it, which can be complex and time-consuming.

Strategies:

- **Data Normalization**: Implement data normalization techniques to standardize data formats and ensure consistency across different sources. This includes converting data into a common format and handling missing or incomplete data.
- **Automated Data Cleaning**: Utilize automated data cleaning tools to identify and correct errors, inconsistencies, and duplicates in the data before feeding it into AI systems.
- **Integration Frameworks**: Use integration frameworks and middleware to streamline the process of aggregating and harmonizing data from disparate sources.

Example:

To handle data variability from different social media platforms, an OSINT system might use a data preprocessing pipeline that standardizes text data, extracts relevant information, and formats it consistently before analysis.

2. Algorithmic Bias and Fairness

Overview:

AI algorithms can exhibit biases based on the data they are trained on, leading to skewed or unfair results. Addressing algorithmic bias is critical to ensuring that AI-enhanced OSINT tools provide accurate and equitable insights.

Challenges:

- **Training Data Bias**: AI models may inherit biases present in the training data, resulting in biased outcomes.
- **Lack of Diversity**: Insufficient diversity in training data can lead to incomplete or skewed representations of various groups or scenarios.

Strategies:

- **Bias Detection**: Implement techniques for detecting and mitigating bias in AI algorithms, such as fairness-aware machine learning methods and regular audits of model outputs.
- **Diverse Training Data**: Use diverse and representative training datasets to reduce bias and improve the generalization of AI models. This includes incorporating data from various sources and demographic groups.
- **Transparency and Documentation**: Maintain transparency about the data used for training and the methodologies employed to address bias. Documenting these processes helps build trust and accountability.

Example:

An OSINT tool analyzing sentiment from social media posts might incorporate techniques to detect and adjust for biases related to language or demographic factors, ensuring more accurate and fair sentiment analysis.

3. System Integration and Compatibility

Overview:

Integrating AI tools into existing OSINT systems and workflows can pose challenges related to system compatibility and seamless operation.

Challenges:

- **Legacy Systems**: Existing OSINT systems may use legacy technologies that are incompatible with modern AI tools.
- **Integration Complexity**: Combining AI tools with current systems can involve complex integration tasks, including API connectivity, data flow management, and user interface adjustments.

Strategies:

- **Modular Architecture**: Adopt a modular architecture for AI integration, allowing new AI tools to be added or replaced without disrupting existing systems. This includes using APIs and microservices for connectivity.
- **Compatibility Testing**: Conduct thorough compatibility testing to ensure that AI tools work seamlessly with existing systems. Address any integration issues before full deployment.
- **Flexible Integration Solutions**: Utilize integration solutions such as middleware or data integration platforms that can bridge gaps between different systems and facilitate smooth interactions.

Example:

Integrating an AI-based analytics tool with a legacy OSINT platform might involve developing custom APIs or using middleware to ensure that data flows smoothly between the two systems.

4. Scalability and Performance

Overview:

As the volume of data and the complexity of analysis increase, ensuring that AI tools scale effectively and maintain high performance is essential for successful OSINT integration.

Challenges:

- **Data Volume**: Handling large volumes of data can strain system resources and affect performance.
- **Processing Speed**: AI algorithms may require significant computational power, impacting processing speed and responsiveness.

Strategies:

- **Scalable Infrastructure**: Implement scalable infrastructure solutions, such as cloud-based platforms or distributed computing, to handle increasing data volumes and processing requirements.
- **Performance Optimization**: Optimize AI algorithms and systems for performance, including techniques such as parallel processing, model optimization, and resource allocation management.

- **Load Balancing**: Use load balancing techniques to distribute computational workloads across multiple servers or instances, ensuring consistent performance and avoiding bottlenecks.

Example:

An OSINT system handling real-time data streams might use cloud-based infrastructure with auto-scaling capabilities to accommodate fluctuations in data volume and maintain optimal performance.

5. Security and Privacy Concerns

Overview:

Integrating AI into OSINT workflows introduces additional security and privacy concerns, including the protection of sensitive data and safeguarding against unauthorized access.

Challenges:

- **Data Security**: Ensuring the security of data collected and processed by AI tools is critical to prevent breaches and unauthorized access.
- **Privacy Risks**: AI systems handling personal or sensitive data must comply with privacy regulations and protect individual privacy.

Strategies:

- **Data Encryption**: Implement strong encryption methods to protect data both in transit and at rest. This includes encrypting sensitive information and securing communication channels.
- **Access Controls**: Establish robust access controls and authentication mechanisms to prevent unauthorized access to AI systems and data.
- **Compliance and Privacy Policies**: Develop and enforce policies to ensure compliance with privacy regulations and best practices. Regularly review and update these policies as needed.

Example:

To address security concerns, an OSINT system might use end-to-end encryption for data transmitted between AI tools and storage systems, along with strict access controls to protect sensitive information.

6. Adaptability and Continuous Improvement

Overview:

AI and OSINT technologies are continually evolving, making it important to maintain adaptability and commit to continuous improvement to keep pace with advancements.

Challenges:

- **Rapid Technological Change**: Keeping up with rapid advancements in AI technology and OSINT methods can be challenging.
- **Evolving Requirements**: OSINT needs and priorities may change over time, requiring ongoing adjustments to AI tools and workflows.

Strategies:

- **Regular Updates**: Keep AI tools and systems up-to-date with the latest advancements and improvements. This includes applying software updates, incorporating new features, and addressing emerging challenges.
- **Feedback Loops**: Establish feedback loops to gather input from users and stakeholders, using this information to refine and enhance AI tools and processes.
- **Innovation and Research**: Invest in research and innovation to stay ahead of technological trends and explore new opportunities for enhancing OSINT capabilities with AI.

Example:

An organization might set up regular review cycles to assess the effectiveness of AI tools, incorporating user feedback and staying informed about new developments to ensure that the system remains cutting-edge.

Overcoming technical challenges in AI-OSINT integration involves addressing issues related to data quality, algorithmic bias, system integration, scalability, security, and adaptability. By implementing strategies such as data normalization, bias detection, modular architecture, scalable infrastructure, and robust security measures, organizations can effectively integrate AI into their OSINT workflows. Continuous improvement and staying current with technological advancements are also crucial for maximizing the benefits of AI and ensuring successful integration.

11.3. Building a Skilled Team for AI-Driven OSINT

Successfully integrating Artificial Intelligence (AI) into Open Source Intelligence (OSINT) workflows relies not only on technology but also on having a skilled team capable of leveraging these tools effectively. Building a team with the right mix of skills and expertise is crucial for optimizing AI-driven OSINT efforts. This section outlines the key steps and considerations for assembling and developing a team to support AI-enhanced OSINT initiatives.

1. Identifying Required Roles and Skills

Overview:

The first step in building a skilled team for AI-driven OSINT is identifying the roles and skills needed to effectively implement and manage AI technologies within OSINT workflows.

Key Roles and Skills:

- **Data Scientists**: Responsible for developing and refining AI models, including machine learning algorithms and natural language processing techniques. Skills in statistical analysis, programming (e.g., Python, R), and machine learning are essential.
- **Data Analysts**: Focus on interpreting and analyzing the data produced by AI tools, deriving actionable insights, and creating reports. Proficiency in data visualization, statistical analysis, and domain knowledge is important.
- **Cybersecurity Experts**: Ensure the security and integrity of data and AI systems. Expertise in cybersecurity protocols, threat analysis, and data protection is crucial.
- **AI/ML Engineers**: Design, build, and maintain AI systems and infrastructure. Skills in AI frameworks (e.g., TensorFlow, PyTorch), software engineering, and cloud computing are necessary.
- **OSINT Specialists**: Provide expertise in gathering and analyzing open-source information. Knowledge of OSINT techniques, tools, and sources is important.

Example:

A successful team for AI-driven OSINT might include a data scientist to develop predictive models, a data analyst to interpret results, a cybersecurity expert to secure the system, and an OSINT specialist to guide the information collection process.

2. Recruiting and Training Talent

Overview:

Attracting and developing skilled professionals is critical for building a team capable of leveraging AI for OSINT. Effective recruitment and ongoing training ensure that the team remains competent and up-to-date with technological advancements.

Recruitment Strategies:

- **Job Descriptions**: Create clear and detailed job descriptions that outline the required skills and responsibilities for each role. Highlight the importance of AI expertise in OSINT contexts.
- **Talent Pools**: Leverage various channels to recruit talent, including industry conferences, job fairs, online platforms (e.g., LinkedIn), and academic institutions.
- **Partnerships**: Partner with universities and research institutions to identify and recruit emerging talent in AI and OSINT fields.

Training and Development:

- **Onboarding**: Provide comprehensive onboarding programs to familiarize new team members with the organization's OSINT processes, AI tools, and specific requirements.
- **Continuous Learning**: Encourage continuous learning through professional development opportunities, such as workshops, online courses, certifications, and industry conferences.
- **Knowledge Sharing**: Foster a culture of knowledge sharing within the team, including regular meetings, collaborative projects, and internal training sessions.

Example:

Recruiting a data scientist with a background in machine learning and providing them with training on specific OSINT tools and techniques can enhance their ability to develop relevant AI models for intelligence gathering.

3. Fostering Collaboration and Communication

Overview:

Effective collaboration and communication among team members are essential for maximizing the potential of AI-driven OSINT. Ensuring that different roles work together seamlessly enhances the overall effectiveness of the team.

Collaboration Strategies:

- **Cross-Functional Teams**: Create cross-functional teams that include members from different roles, such as data scientists, analysts, and OSINT specialists, to work on projects and share expertise.
- **Project Management**: Implement project management tools and methodologies to facilitate coordination, track progress, and manage tasks across different team members.
- **Regular Meetings**: Hold regular team meetings to discuss ongoing projects, share updates, address challenges, and align on objectives.

Communication Strategies:

- **Clear Channels**: Establish clear communication channels and protocols to ensure that information is shared effectively among team members.
- **Documentation**: Maintain thorough documentation of processes, models, and methodologies to ensure that knowledge is captured and can be referenced by the team.
- **Feedback Mechanisms**: Implement feedback mechanisms to gather input from team members, address concerns, and continuously improve collaboration and communication.

Example:

A project team consisting of a data scientist, an OSINT specialist, and a data analyst might use collaboration tools such as Slack for communication, JIRA for project management, and Confluence for documentation.

4. Ensuring Alignment with Organizational Goals

Overview:

Aligning the team's efforts with the organization's overall goals and strategies ensures that AI-driven OSINT initiatives contribute effectively to broader objectives.

Alignment Strategies:

- **Goal Setting**: Clearly define and communicate the goals and objectives of AI-driven OSINT projects to the team, ensuring that everyone understands how their work supports organizational priorities.
- **Performance Metrics**: Establish performance metrics to measure the impact of AI-driven OSINT efforts on achieving organizational goals. Use these metrics to guide decision-making and adjustments.
- **Strategic Planning**: Involve team members in strategic planning to ensure that their insights and expertise are considered in shaping the direction of AI-driven OSINT initiatives.

Example:

Aligning an AI-driven threat detection project with the organization's cybersecurity strategy ensures that the team's efforts contribute to protecting against emerging threats and enhancing overall security.

5. Managing and Retaining Talent

Overview:

Managing and retaining skilled team members is crucial for maintaining a high-performing team and ensuring long-term success in AI-driven OSINT initiatives.

Management Strategies:

- **Career Development**: Provide opportunities for career advancement and professional growth, such as promotions, additional responsibilities, and leadership roles.
- **Recognition and Rewards**: Recognize and reward the contributions of team members through incentives, awards, and positive feedback.

- **Work Environment**: Create a supportive and engaging work environment that fosters job satisfaction, collaboration, and innovation.

Retention Strategies:

- **Competitive Compensation**: Offer competitive salaries and benefits to attract and retain top talent.
- **Work-Life Balance**: Promote work-life balance by providing flexible work arrangements, such as remote work options or flexible hours.
- **Employee Engagement**: Engage with employees regularly to understand their needs, address concerns, and maintain high levels of motivation and satisfaction.

Example:

Implementing a career development plan that includes opportunities for skill enhancement and leadership growth can help retain talented individuals and keep them motivated.

6. Leveraging External Expertise

Overview:

In addition to building an internal team, leveraging external expertise can provide valuable insights and support for AI-driven OSINT initiatives.

External Expertise Strategies:

- **Consultants**: Engage external consultants or experts in AI and OSINT to provide specialized knowledge, assist with complex projects, or offer strategic guidance.
- **Partnerships**: Form partnerships with academic institutions, research organizations, or industry groups to access cutting-edge research and emerging trends.
- **Vendor Support**: Utilize vendor support services for AI tools and platforms to ensure effective implementation and troubleshooting.

Example:

Collaborating with a university specializing in AI research can provide access to advanced methodologies and innovations that enhance the capabilities of your AI-driven OSINT tools.

Building a skilled team for AI-driven OSINT involves identifying key roles and skills, recruiting and training talent, fostering collaboration and communication, ensuring alignment with organizational goals, managing and retaining talent, and leveraging external expertise. By focusing on these areas, organizations can create a competent and motivated team capable of effectively integrating AI into OSINT workflows, driving innovation, and achieving intelligence objectives.

11.4. Measuring the Success of AI-OSINT Implementations

Measuring the success of AI-enhanced Open Source Intelligence (OSINT) implementations is essential to evaluate their effectiveness, efficiency, and overall impact on organizational goals. Effective measurement helps identify areas for improvement, justify investments, and demonstrate the value of AI in OSINT activities. This section outlines key metrics, methods, and considerations for assessing the success of AI-OSINT implementations.

1. Defining Success Criteria

Overview:

Before measuring success, it is crucial to define clear and specific criteria that align with the objectives of the AI-OSINT implementation. Success criteria should reflect both the performance of the AI tools and the impact on OSINT goals.

Criteria Examples:

- **Accuracy and Reliability**: The precision and correctness of the AI models in analyzing and interpreting data.
- **Efficiency Gains**: Improvements in the speed and resource usage of OSINT processes due to AI integration.
- **Actionable Insights**: The relevance and usefulness of the insights generated by AI tools in supporting decision-making.
- **User Satisfaction**: The level of satisfaction among users interacting with AI-enhanced OSINT systems.

Example:

If the objective is to enhance threat detection, success criteria might include a reduction in false positives and false negatives, faster identification of threats, and positive feedback from cybersecurity analysts.

2. Key Performance Indicators (KPIs)

Overview:

Key Performance Indicators (KPIs) are specific metrics used to quantify the success of AI-OSINT implementations. KPIs should be aligned with the defined success criteria and provide actionable insights into performance.

KPIs Examples:

- **Detection Accuracy**: Measures the percentage of correctly identified threats or relevant information by AI tools.
- **Processing Speed**: Evaluates the time taken by AI systems to process and analyze data.
- **False Positive/Negative Rates**: Assesses the rate of incorrect classifications or predictions made by AI models.
- **User Adoption Rate**: Tracks the extent to which users are utilizing the AI-enhanced OSINT tools.
- **Cost Savings**: Calculates the reduction in costs due to increased efficiency and automation provided by AI.

Example:

A KPI for a real-time threat detection system might include metrics such as the average time to detect and respond to threats, the accuracy of threat classifications, and user satisfaction with the system's alerts.

3. Evaluation Methods

Overview:

Various methods can be employed to evaluate the performance and success of AI-OSINT implementations. These methods provide quantitative and qualitative insights into how well the AI tools are achieving their intended goals.

Evaluation Methods:

- **Benchmarking**: Compare the performance of AI-enhanced OSINT tools against industry standards or similar systems to assess their effectiveness.
- **Performance Testing**: Conduct controlled tests to measure the accuracy, speed, and reliability of AI models using predefined datasets.
- **User Feedback**: Gather feedback from users to evaluate their satisfaction, ease of use, and perceived value of the AI tools.
- **Impact Analysis**: Assess the impact of AI tools on achieving specific OSINT objectives, such as improved threat detection or enhanced data analysis capabilities.

Example:

Performance testing for a sentiment analysis tool might involve using a labeled dataset to evaluate the accuracy of sentiment classifications and comparing the results to benchmarks established by similar tools.

4. Analyzing and Interpreting Results

Overview:

After collecting performance data and feedback, analyzing and interpreting the results is crucial for understanding the effectiveness of AI-OSINT implementations and identifying areas for improvement.

Analysis Techniques:

- **Data Analysis**: Use statistical and analytical methods to interpret performance metrics, identify trends, and assess the overall effectiveness of AI tools.
- **Comparison with Benchmarks**: Compare results against benchmarks or industry standards to determine how well the AI tools are performing relative to expectations.
- **Root Cause Analysis**: Investigate any issues or anomalies to understand their root causes and develop solutions for improvement.

Example:

If the analysis reveals a high false positive rate in a threat detection system, conducting a root cause analysis might uncover issues with the training data or model parameters, leading to targeted adjustments to improve accuracy.

5. Continuous Improvement and Iteration

Overview:

Measuring success is an ongoing process that should feed into continuous improvement efforts. Iterative improvements ensure that AI-OSINT tools remain effective and relevant over time.

Continuous Improvement Strategies:

- **Feedback Integration**: Regularly incorporate user feedback and performance data to make iterative improvements to AI models and processes.
- **Model Retraining**: Periodically retrain AI models with updated data to enhance accuracy and adapt to evolving trends.
- **Process Optimization**: Identify and address inefficiencies in OSINT workflows to maximize the benefits of AI integration.

Example:

A machine learning model used for detecting malicious activity might be retrained with new data to adapt to emerging threats, improving its accuracy and relevance over time.

6. Reporting and Communication

Overview:

Effectively communicating the results of AI-OSINT evaluations is important for demonstrating value, justifying investments, and aligning stakeholders with the outcomes of AI initiatives.

Reporting Strategies:

- **Performance Reports**: Create detailed reports that summarize key metrics, findings, and insights from the evaluation process. Include visualizations and comparisons to convey results clearly.
- **Stakeholder Communication**: Present findings to stakeholders, including management, team members, and other relevant parties, to highlight the impact of AI-OSINT implementations and discuss any recommended improvements.

- **Success Stories**: Share success stories and case studies that illustrate the benefits and positive outcomes of AI integration in OSINT workflows.

Example:

A performance report for an AI-enhanced OSINT tool might include charts and graphs showing improvements in detection accuracy, user adoption rates, and cost savings, along with a summary of user feedback and recommendations for future enhancements.

Measuring the success of AI-OSINT implementations involves defining success criteria, selecting relevant KPIs, employing evaluation methods, analyzing results, and driving continuous improvement. By systematically assessing the performance and impact of AI tools, organizations can ensure that their AI-driven OSINT efforts are effective, efficient, and aligned with strategic goals. Effective reporting and communication of results further support informed decision-making and demonstrate the value of AI in enhancing OSINT capabilities.

11.5. Adapting to the Constantly Evolving AI Landscape

In the dynamic field of AI, where technologies and methodologies evolve rapidly, staying adaptable is crucial for maintaining the effectiveness of AI-enhanced Open Source Intelligence (OSINT) implementations. This section explores strategies for navigating and leveraging the continuously changing AI landscape to ensure that AI-OSINT systems remain current, relevant, and capable of addressing emerging challenges.

1. Staying Informed About AI Trends

Overview:

Keeping up with the latest developments in AI technologies, methodologies, and best practices is essential for adapting AI-OSINT implementations to the evolving landscape.

Strategies for Staying Informed:

- **Industry News and Journals**: Regularly read industry news, academic journals, and research papers to stay updated on the latest advancements in AI and OSINT.

- **Conferences and Workshops**: Attend AI and cybersecurity conferences, workshops, and seminars to learn about emerging trends, technologies, and best practices from experts and peers.
- **Professional Networks**: Engage with professional networks, forums, and online communities to exchange knowledge, share experiences, and gain insights from other practitioners in the field.

Example:

Subscribing to AI research journals and attending annual cybersecurity conferences can provide valuable insights into new AI techniques and their potential applications in OSINT.

2. Evaluating and Integrating New AI Technologies

Overview:

As new AI technologies and tools emerge, evaluating their potential benefits and integrating them into existing OSINT workflows can enhance capabilities and maintain competitiveness.

Evaluation Process:

- **Technology Assessment**: Assess the capabilities, strengths, and limitations of new AI technologies to determine their relevance and potential impact on OSINT activities.
- **Pilot Testing**: Conduct pilot tests or proof-of-concept projects to evaluate the performance and effectiveness of new AI tools in real-world scenarios before full-scale integration.
- **Vendor Analysis**: Evaluate vendors and solution providers to ensure that they offer robust, reliable, and compatible AI technologies for OSINT applications.

Integration Strategies:

- **Modular Integration**: Integrate new AI technologies in a modular fashion to minimize disruption to existing systems and allow for gradual adoption.
- **Training and Support**: Provide training and support to ensure that team members can effectively use new AI tools and technologies.
- **Feedback Loop**: Establish a feedback loop to gather insights from users and make necessary adjustments to optimize the integration of new technologies.

Example:

Integrating a new machine learning algorithm for sentiment analysis may involve pilot testing the algorithm with historical data, evaluating its performance, and then training the team to use it effectively in real-time analysis.

3. Maintaining Flexibility in AI-OSINT Workflows

Overview:

Flexibility in workflows allows organizations to quickly adapt to changes in AI technology and evolving intelligence needs, ensuring that OSINT processes remain effective and responsive.

Flexibility Strategies:

- **Scalable Architecture**: Design AI-OSINT systems with scalable architectures that can accommodate new technologies, increased data volumes, and evolving requirements.
- **Modular Design**: Implement modular design principles to enable the easy addition or replacement of components and technologies within the OSINT workflow.
- **Regular Reviews**: Conduct regular reviews of AI-OSINT workflows to identify areas for improvement, address emerging challenges, and incorporate new technologies.

Example:

Using a modular AI architecture allows an organization to seamlessly integrate new data sources or analytical tools without overhauling the entire OSINT system.

4. Enhancing Collaboration with AI Innovators

Overview:

Collaborating with AI researchers, innovators, and technology providers can provide valuable insights and access to cutting-edge solutions that enhance AI-OSINT capabilities.

Collaboration Opportunities:

- **Research Partnerships**: Partner with academic institutions and research organizations to explore new AI methodologies and contribute to collaborative research projects.
- **Technology Alliances**: Form alliances with technology providers and vendors to gain early access to emerging AI tools and technologies.
- **Innovation Hubs**: Engage with innovation hubs, incubators, and startups to explore novel AI solutions and stay ahead of technological trends.

Example:

Collaborating with a research university on a joint project can provide access to experimental AI techniques and methodologies that may be applied to enhance OSINT capabilities.

5. Preparing for AI-Related Challenges

Overview:

As AI technologies evolve, new challenges may arise, including ethical considerations, security risks, and technical limitations. Proactively addressing these challenges is essential for maintaining effective AI-OSINT implementations.

Challenge Preparation Strategies:

- **Risk Management**: Identify potential risks associated with new AI technologies, such as security vulnerabilities or ethical concerns, and develop mitigation strategies.
- **Ethical Guidelines**: Stay informed about ethical guidelines and best practices for AI use, and ensure that new technologies are aligned with ethical standards.
- **Security Measures**: Implement robust security measures to protect AI systems from threats and vulnerabilities, and regularly update security protocols to address emerging risks.

Example:

Implementing strong encryption and access controls for AI systems can mitigate security risks and ensure that sensitive data remains protected.

6. Fostering a Culture of Continuous Improvement

Overview:

Promoting a culture of continuous improvement encourages ongoing learning, adaptation, and innovation, helping organizations stay agile in the face of evolving AI technologies.

Cultural Strategies:

- **Encourage Innovation**: Foster an environment where team members are encouraged to explore new ideas, experiment with emerging technologies, and propose innovative solutions.
- **Support Learning**: Provide opportunities for ongoing professional development and training to keep team members updated on the latest AI advancements and best practices.
- **Promote Adaptability**: Cultivate a mindset of adaptability and flexibility, where team members are open to change and willing to embrace new technologies and methodologies.

Example:

Encouraging team members to participate in AI hackathons or innovation challenges can stimulate creativity and lead to the development of new approaches for integrating AI into OSINT workflows.

Adapting to the constantly evolving AI landscape involves staying informed about AI trends, evaluating and integrating new technologies, maintaining flexibility in workflows, collaborating with AI innovators, preparing for challenges, and fostering a culture of continuous improvement. By implementing these strategies, organizations can ensure that their AI-driven OSINT systems remain effective, relevant, and capable of addressing emerging threats and opportunities in the rapidly changing world of AI.

In a world where cyber threats are constantly evolving, the ability to gather, analyze, and act on intelligence is more crucial than ever. "*AI and OSINT: The Future of Cyber Investigation*" explores the groundbreaking integration of Artificial Intelligence (AI) with Open Source Intelligence (OSINT), offering readers a glimpse into the future of cyber investigations.

This comprehensive guide takes you on a journey through the history and evolution of OSINT, highlighting its pivotal role in cybersecurity and its transformation through AI. The book delves into the latest AI techniques that are enhancing OSINT practices, from machine learning and natural language processing to real-time threat detection and predictive analytics.

Readers will discover a wealth of AI-driven OSINT tools, each designed to tackle the challenges of today's complex digital landscape. Through real-world case studies and practical insights, the book demonstrates how AI is not just augmenting traditional OSINT methods but revolutionizing the entire field.

Beyond the technical aspects, "AI and OSINT" addresses the ethical, legal, and regulatory challenges that come with integrating AI into cyber investigations. It provides a roadmap for professionals looking to implement AI-driven OSINT strategies within their organizations, balancing automation with human expertise.

As the digital world continues to expand, so too does the need for innovative solutions to protect against cyber threats. "AI and OSINT: The Future of Cyber Investigation" equips readers with the knowledge and tools to stay ahead of the curve, offering a forward-looking perspective on the future of cybersecurity and intelligence gathering.

Whether you are a seasoned cybersecurity professional, a law enforcement officer, or simply interested in the cutting-edge of digital intelligence, this book is an essential resource for understanding how AI is shaping the future of cyber investigations.